INTRODUCTION TO JUDAISM:

A COURSE OUTLINE

*This book was made possible through
the generosity of the following donors
to the*

UAHC FUND FOR REFORM JUDAISM

Sondra and Louis Bell
Shelli and Herbert Dodell
Lorraine and Jerry Factor
Evelyn and Norman Feintech
Eris and Larry Field
Shirley Firestein
Shirley and Joseph Kleiman
Haya and Paul Reisbord
Lily and Donald Rosman
Janet and Maxwell Salter
Sandra and Mitchell Shames
Edith and Harold Swerdlow
Helen and David Weinstein
Rita and Theodore Williams
Marilyn and Sigi Ziering

איחוד
ליהדות
מתקדמת
באמריקה

INTRODUCTION TO JUDAISM:

A Course Outline

Compiled and Edited by
RABBI STEPHEN J. EINSTEIN
and LYDIA KUKOFF

כֹּל אֲשֶׁר־דִּבֶּר יְהֹוָה נַעֲשֶׂה וְנִשְׁמָע

*"All that the Lord has spoken we shall do
and we shall hear."*   Exodus 24:7

UNION OF AMERICAN HEBREW CONGREGATIONS
New York

Library of Congress Cataloging in Publication Data

Einstein, Stephen J.
Introduction to Judaism.

Bibliography: p.
1. Judaism—Customs and practices—Outlines,
syllabi, etc. I. Kukoff, Lydia. II. Union of American
Hebrew Congregations. III. Title.
BM700.E34 1983 296 83-3536
ISBN 0-8074-0251-6

Contents

Foreword

One of the most refreshing developments in the North American Jewish community has been the growing emphasis on adult Jewish learning and experience. A whole generation of Jews whose Jewish education may have ended with Bar/Bat Mitzvah or confirmation are seeking to reclaim their heritage. In addition, in large measure because of the UAHC's Outreach Program, increasing numbers of men and women born into other faiths have determined to study Judaism and to consider Judaism as their personal religion.

Introduction to Judaism: A Course Outline is an ideal tool with which to acquaint both born Jews and those considering Judaism with what it means to "do Jewishly." It involves the student in rituals, life-cycle observances, home celebrations, music, and even cooking.

We extend our thanks to Rabbi Stephen J. Einstein, Lydia Kukoff, and those who helped create and shape this volume. Active rather than passive, field tested for three years with over five hundred adult participants, *Introduction to Judaism* is a central component of adult education and introduction to Judaism programs throughout the North American Jewish community.

Rabbi Daniel B. Syme
Director of Education

Acknowledgments

There are many people who have participated in the creation of this course outline. We wish to acknowledge their contribution though no words can adequately thank them for the devotion that they have shown to this project:

Rabbi Erwin L. Herman who entrusted us with the task of bringing this course outline into being. He shared his wisdom with us while at the same time allowing us the freedom that creativity requires.

Rabbi Daniel B. Syme who taught us the process of building a new course and who has guided this project to its completion.

The task force of talented rabbis and educators who gave hours and hours of their time and expertise in the creation of the individual lesson plans—Judy Aronson, Sherry Bissell, Elissa Blaser, Rabbi Bruce Block, Rabbi Jerrold Goldstein, Rabbi Eli Herscher, Rabbi Elliot J. Holin, Lynda Rocklin, Hildy Sheinman, and Linda Thal.

The instructors and students of the UAHC's Introduction to Judaism course in the Greater Los Angeles area whose evaluations were invaluable in the final editing of this course outline.

Dr. William Cutter, Victoria Kelman, and Sara Lee for their counsel during the initial stages of this project.

Rabbi Lawrence Jackofsky for sharing with us his material on the structure of the Bible and the service.

Rabbi Roland B. Gittelsohn for allowing us to utilize some of his material, adding perspective to this study.

Robin Einstein, Selma Einstein ז״ל , Tova Halperin, Victoria Kelman, and Mildred Kessler for their contributions which added to the experiential portions of the course.

Cheryl Sortor and Debbie Villepigue for their clerical assistance.

Robin Einstein for her painstaking attention to detail in the preparation of the final manuscript.

Rabbi Alexander M. Schindler for his encouragement and support.

And, finally, to Robin Einstein and Ben Kukoff who have shared our delight and enthusiasm in the creation of this course outline.

List of Books and Materials for the Course

1. Notebook with materials for each unit.
2. Jewish calendar.
3. *The Torah: A Modern Commentary,* by W. Gunther Plaut and Bernard J. Bamberger, with essays by William W. Hallo (New York: Union of American Hebrew Congregations, 1981).
4. *The Holy Scriptures* (Philadelphia: Jewish Publication Society of America, 1955).
5. *Gates of Prayer* (New York: Central Conference of American Rabbis, 1975).
6. *A Shabbat Manual* and tape (New York: Central Conference of American Rabbis, 1972).
7. A history book such as *The Story of Judaism,* by Bernard J. Bamberger (New York: Schocken Books, 1970), or *Jews, God, and History,* by Max I. Dimont (New York: New American Library, Inc., Signet Book, 1962).
8. *The Passover Seder: Pathways through the Haggadah,* by Arthur Gilbert (New York: Ktav Publishing Co., 1965).
9. *Alef-Bet: A Hebrew Primer,* by Abraham and Adaia Shumsky (New York: Union of American Hebrew Congregations, 1979).
10. *Choosing Judaism,* by Lydia Kukoff (New York: Union of American Hebrew Congregations, 1981).
11. *The Jewish Home,* Books 1–10, by Daniel B. Syme (New York: Union of American Hebrew Congregations).
12. *Keeping Posted,* edited by Aron Hirt-Manheimer (unless otherwise indicated) (New York: Union of American Hebrew Congregations).

What to Bring to Class

1. The Jewish calendar, Bible, prayer book, and notebook are to be brought to *each* class.
2. *A Shabbat Manual* should be brought *only* to the two classes which deal with *Shabbat.*
3. *The Passover Seder: Pathways through the Haggadah* should be brought *only* to the classes dealing with *Pesach.*
4. The *Shabbat* tape and the history book are to be used at home and need not be brought to class.

List of Journal Entries

For your convenience, Journal entries occurring in each lesson are listed below. When students have missed a lesson (consisting of resource sheets), they should see the instructor to obtain make-up material, as well as to get the Journal entries and any other assignment which they missed.

BEGINNINGS

Write a brief statement or sketch of your feelings as you begin this class.

BIRTH
No Journal entries.

CHANUKAH
Record in your Journal your feelings about the distinction between light and darkness as the light increases.

CONVERSION
1. What were your initial reasons for coming to this basic Judaism class?
2. If you are considering conversion, what are your reasons for conversion at this point?
3. What Hebrew name will you choose? Why?

DEATH
No Journal entries.

JEWISH EDUCATION
1. Make two life-cycle charts, one showing the ceremonies which have marked the important milestones in your life and one showing the life-cycle ceremonies you expect your children to celebrate.

2. As you continue your own Jewish education, about what things would you like to learn more? Why?

MARRIAGE
1. Listen to the song "Do You Love Me?" from *Fiddler on the Roof* and respond to these questions: Why did Tevye and Golda get married? Why do people get married today?
2. In what ways might you make your home more Jewish?

PESACH
No Journal entries.

PURIM
1. For what would you be willing to risk your life?
2. Considering the realities of history, what would be your reasons for wanting your children to be Jewish?

ROSH HASHANAH
Jot down in your Journal one dream you have for yourself and how you can make that dream come true.

SHABBAT—PART I
Make two lists in your Journal, one list of those things in your life that are ordinary and one list of the extraordinary.

SHABBAT—PART II
After *Shabbat,* write in your Journal your feelings about the two things you did or did not do (from Resource Sheet 55—"Chart of Possibilities and Beginnings").

SHAVUOT
No Journal entries.

SIMCHAT TORAH
Read "Carrying Around the Torah" (Resource Sheet 65). Record your feelings about the story.

SUKOT
1. Make a list of Jewish guests, past or present, whom you would invite to your *sukah.*
2. Of the four types of people described in *"Midrash Leviticus Rabbah* 30:12" (Resource Sheet 71), which one do you most resemble?

YOM HA'ATSMAUT
No Journal entries.

YOM HASHOAH

1. You may hear Jews say, "You didn't experience the Holocaust. How can you understand it? How can you possibly know how it feels?" How might you feel, hearing that question? How might you respond?

2. At the moment of conversion, one promises to cast one's lot with that of the Jewish people. What are the implications of "Casting one's lot with the Jewish people"? Given what you know of the Holocaust and the history of anti-Semitism, why would a Jew *choose* to remain Jewish?

YOM KIPPUR

1. What is one thing I did this year which I liked?

2. What is one thing I did this year which I would do differently?

Make-Up Readings

Write a report on the reading. (If you would prefer to read a book or selection not mentioned here, check with your instructor.)

1. *Birth*

Read *The Jewish Home,* Book 7, and all the other material on "Birth" in the notebook.

2. *Chanukah*

Read *The Jewish Home,* Book 3, on *"Chanukah."* Read all other material on *"Chanukah"* in the notebook.

Or read three selections from *The Hanukkah Anthology,* edited by Philip Goodman (Philadelphia: Jewish Publication Society of America, 1976).

3. *Conversion*

Read Jews-by-choice material and all other material on "Conversion" in the notebook.

Or read *Choosing Judaism,* by Lydia Kukoff.

4. *Death*

Read all selections on "Death" in the notebook *plus* the section on "Death and Burial" in *The Jewish Catalog,* Vol. I, pp. 172–181, edited by Richard Siegel, Michael Strassfeld, and Sharon Strassfeld (Philadelphia: Jewish Publication Society of America, 1973).

5. *Jewish Education*

Read *The Jewish Home,* Book 8, on *"Bar/Bat Mitzvah"* and "Confirmation" *plus* other material in "Jewish Education" in the notebook.

6. *Marriage*

Read *The Jewish Home,* Books 9 and 10, on "Marriage" *plus* other material in the notebook and the section on "Weddings" in *The Jewish Catalog,* Vol. I, pp. 158–166.

7. *Pesach*

Read *The Jewish Home,* Book 2, on *"Pesach" plus* other material in the notebook and explanatory material in *The Passover Seder: Pathways through the Haggadah.*

8. *Purim*

Read *The Jewish Home,* Book 3, on *"Purim" plus* all other material in the *"Purim"* section of the notebook.

9. *Rosh Hashanah*

Read *The Jewish Home,* Book 4, on the "High Holy Days" *plus* all other material on *"Rosh Hashanah"* in the notebook.

10. *Shabbat*

Read *The Jewish Home,* Book 1, on *"Shabbat" plus* all other material on *"Shabbat*—Part I" and *"Shabbat*—Part II" in the notebook and pp. 5–6 and 70–80 in *A Shabbat Manual.*

11. *Shavuot*

Read *The Jewish Home,* Book 5, *plus* all other material in the *"Shavuot"* section in the notebook.

12. *Simchat Torah*

Read *The Jewish Home,* Book 6, *plus* all other material in the *"Simchat Torah"* section of the notebook.

13. *Sukot*

Read *The Jewish Home,* Book 6, *plus* all other material on *"Sukot"* in the notebook. Also fill in Resource Sheet 67 ("Family Tree").

14. *Yom Ha'atsmaut*

Read one of the following:

Exodus, by Leon Uris (New York: Doubleday and Co., 1958).

The Source, by James A. Michener (New York: Fawcett, 1978).

A History of Israel: From the Rise of Zionism to Our Time, by Howard M. Sachar (New York: Knopf, 1979). Read several chapters.

15. *Yom Hashoah*

Read one of the following:

The Diary of a Young Girl, by Anne Frank (New York: Doubleday and Co., 1967).

Anya, by Susan Fromberg Shaffer (New York: Macmillan, 1974).

Mila 18, by Leon Uris (New York: Doubleday, 1961).

Morning Stars, by Zalman Shazar (Philadelphia: Jewish Publication Society of America, 1967).

The War Against the Jews 1933–1945, by Lucy Dawidowicz (New York: Bantam, 1976).

Life Is with People, by Elizabeth Herzog and Mark Zborowski (New York: Schocken, 1952).

Any book by Sholom Aleichem, I.L. Peretz, or Isaac Bashevis Singer.

16. *Yom Kippur*

Read *The Jewish Home,* Book 4, on the "High Holy Days" *plus* all other material on *"Yom Kippur"* in the notebook.

Bibliography

This is a selected bibliography. A more extensive bibliography can be found in *Choosing Judaism,* by Lydia Kukoff (New York: Union of American Hebrew Congregations, 1981), pp. 132–150.

ANTI-SEMITISM

Reuther, Rosemary. *Faith and Fratricide.* Seabury Press, 1974.
    A brilliant study of the theological roots of anti-Semitism.

Sartre, Jean-Paul. *Anti-Semite and Jew.* Translated from the French by George J. Becker. Schocken, 1948.
    A brilliant portrait of both anti-Semite and Jew written by a non-Jew from a non-Jewish point of view.

BIBLE

The Prophets, Nevi'im: A New Translation of the Holy Scriptures According to the Traditional Hebrew Text. Jewish Publication Society of America, 1978.
    A new English translation of the major and minor prophets rendered in accurate, fluent, and idiomatic fashion.

Sandmel, Samuel. *The Enjoyment of Scripture: The Law, the Prophets, and the Writings.* Oxford University Press, 1974.
    Concerned with the literary method and quality of the various kinds of writings found in the *Tanach.*

The Torah: The Five Books of Moses. Jewish Publication Society of America, 1962.
    A scholarly and readable English translation of the Pentateuch taking into account the latest linguistic researches and archeological discoveries.

The Torah: A Modern Commentary. Commentaries by W. Gunther Plaut and Bernard J. Bamberger. Union of American Hebrew Congregations, 1981.

This first major Reform commentary on the Five Books of Moses contains the Hebrew text, the new translation by the Jewish Publication Society, incisive commentary, and related writings from an encyclopedic range of sources. Also included are the *haftarot* for each *sidrah* and for special days.

The Writings, Ketubim: A New Translation of the Holy Scriptures According to the Traditional Hebrew Text. Jewish Publication Society of America, 1982.

An accurate, readable new English translation of the third section of the Hebrew Bible.

BRANCHES OF JUDAISM

Keeping Posted. Volume XXVI, Number 3, December 1980, "Conservative Judaism."
Volume XXV, Number 4, January 1980, "Orthodox Judaism."
Volume XXVII, Number 3, January 1982, "Reconstructionism."
Volume XXIV, Number 1, September 1978, "What Is Reform?"

Segal, Abraham. *One People.* Union of American Hebrew Congregations, 1982.

A textbook-workbook dealing with the misconceptions about Judaism's main branches, the differences that separate them, and the similarities that make them one people.

CHRISTIANITY AND JUDAISM

Keeping Posted. Edited by Edith Samuel. Volume XIX, Number 3, December 1973, "Judaism and Christianity: The Parting of the Ways."

Sandmel, Samuel. *We Jews and Jesus.* Oxford University Press, 1973.

Written in a nontechnical style for the layperson, this book describes the what and why of the Jewish attitude to Jesus.

Silver, Abba Hillel. *Where Judaism Differed.* Macmillan, 1956.

A lively account of the distinctive values and outlook of Judaism and an exploration of the sharp divergencies between Judaism and Christianity.

Weiss-Rosmarin, Trude. *Judaism and Christianity: The Differences.* Jonathan David, 1965.

Concise, popular presentation of the teachings of and differences between Judaism and Christianity.

FICTION

Bellow, Saul, ed. *Great Jewish Short Stories.* Dell, 1963.

Representative selections from the short stories of the most prominent Jewish authors of the last century. Includes writings of Agnon, Bellow, Singer, Babel, Peretz, and others.

Michener, James A. *The Source.* Fawcett, 1978.

A remarkable novel which skillfully recounts thousands of years of history in Israel through the wonders of archeology.

Schwarz, Leo W., ed. *The Jewish Caravan: Great Stories of Twenty-five Centuries.* Schocken, 1976.

Vast selection of Jewish writing, both ancient and modern. Includes such literary giants as S.Y. Agnon, Sholom Aleichem, Franz Kafka, I. B. Singer, and Isaac Babel.

Wiesel, Elie. *Souls on Fire: Portraits and Legends of Hasidic Masters.* Random House, 1973.

Delightful retelling of the tales of the chasidic masters of the eighteenth and nineteenth centuries. Includes portraits of Israel Baal Shem Tov, Levi Yitzhak of Berditchev, and Nachman of Bratzlav.

FOOD

Engle, Fannie, and Blair, Gertrude. *The Jewish Festival Cookbook.* Warner Paperback Library, 1954.

Recipes and menus for all the Jewish holidays as well as a description of holiday customs.

Gethers, Judith, and Lefft, Elizabeth. *The World-Famous Ratner's Meatless Cookbook.* Bantam Books, 1975.

Authentic recipes from Ratner's Dairy Restaurant in New York.

Grossinger, Jennie. *The Art of Jewish Cooking.* Bantam Books, 1958.

Over 300 traditional recipes from an expert on Jewish cooking.

Nathan, Joan. *The Jewish Holiday Kitchen.* Schocken, 1979.

A presentation of the history, food requirements, and traditions of each of the Jewish holidays along with a collection of recipes.

Rockland, Mae S. *The Jewish Party Book: A Contemporary Guide to Customs, Crafts, and Foods.* Schocken, 1979.

Hundreds of recipes, music, and crafts projects for gifts and decorations for every kind of Jewish celebration.

GENERAL

Latner, Helen. *The Book of Modern Jewish Etiquette.* Schocken, 1981.

A compendium of information relating to all aspects of Jewish living.

Samuel, Edith. *Your Jewish Lexicon.* Union of American Hebrew Congregations, 1982.

A clear, concise exploration of basic Hebrew words and concepts.

Steinberg, Milton. *Basic Judaism.* Harcourt, Brace and World, 1947.

An outstanding treatment of the fundamentals of Judaism.

Zborowski, Mark, and Herzog, Elizabeth. *Life Is with People: The Culture of the Shtetl.* Schocken, 1962.

Anthropological study of the world of Eastern European Jewry dealing with, among other things, the Sabbath, *tsedakah,* marriage, and the Jewish home.

GOD

Keeping Posted. Volume XXV, Number 3, December 1979, "Jewish Views of God."

HISTORY

Bamberger, Bernard J. *The Story of Judaism.* Schocken, 1964.

Over 3,000 years of Jewish existence distilled into a single readable volume.

Eisenberg, Azriel; Goodman, Hannah Grad; and Kass, Alvin. *Eyewitnesses to Jewish History: From 486* B.C.E. *to 1967.* Union of American Hebrew Congregations, 1972.

Collection of first-hand reports by people who themselves lived through major events in Jewish history. Some of the events "witnessed" include the revolt of the Maccabees, the Spanish Inquisition, the uprising in the Warsaw Ghetto, and the capture of Eichmann.

Roth, Cecil. *A History of the Jews: From Earliest Times through the Six Day War.* Revised edition. Schocken, 1970.

Popular history tracing the social, religious, and cultural development of the Jewish people from the biblical era down to the present.

Sachar, Abram L. *History of the Jews.* Knopf, 1967.

A complete history of thirty centuries of Judaism, in which due emphasis is given to the economic, social, and environmental factors, as well as to religious and philosophical development.

Sachar, Howard M. *The Course of Modern Jewish History.* Dell, 1977.

Comprehensive and scholarly account of the Jews from the French Revolution to the present day. Depicts the social and cultural influences—both Jewish and non-Jewish—that have formed the civilization of Jews throughout the world.

Seltzer, Robert M. *Jewish People, Jewish Thought: The Jewish Experience in History.* Macmillan, 1980.

Comprehensive one-volume overview of the Jewish people's social and political history set against the intellectual, religious, and cultural currents of the times and places in which Jews lived. An ambitious work, complete with maps, illustrations, and photographs.

HOLIDAYS, FESTIVALS, AND THE SABBATH

Agnon, Shmuel Y. *The Days of Awe.* Schocken, 1965.

Agnon's classic anthology of Jewish wisdom, skillfully crafted as a literary tone poem on the High Holy Days.

Bearman, Jane. *The Eight Nights: A Chanukah Counting Book.* Union of American Hebrew Congregations, 1979.

A lively rhyme for each of the eight nights and exquisite full-color graphics present all the delights of *Chanukah*—lighting candles, singing songs, playing *dreidel,* eating *latkes,* and giving and receiving presents. An imaginative activity book for the very young

Bin-Nun, Judith, and Einhorn, Franne. *Rosh Hashanah: A Holiday Funtext.* Union of American Hebrew Congregations, 1978.

A book about *Rosh Hashanah* for young children encouraging their creative participation.

Cashman, Greer Fay. *Jewish Days and Holidays.* SBS International, 1979.
A lavishly illustrated book for children depicting the joy and celebration of the Jewish holidays.

Gaster, Theodor H. *Festivals of the Jewish Year.* William Sloane Assoc., 1953.
The origins, rituals, customs, and contemporary meaning of the Jewish festivals, fasts, and holy days.

Goodman, Philip, ed. *The Hanukkah Anthology.* Jewish Publication Society of America, 1976.
The seven holiday anthologies edited by Philip Goodman are useful guides for meaningful celebration. Each volume contains sections on the history of the holiday and its observance, the representation of the day in art, poetry and prose readings from both the ancient and modern sources, and the music associated with the celebration.

Goodman, Philip, ed. *The Passover Anthology.* Jewish Publication Society of America, 1961.

Goodman, Philip, ed. *The Purim Anthology.* Jewish Publication Society of America, 1949.

Goodman, Philip, ed. *The Rosh Hashanah Anthology.* Jewish Publication Society of America, 1970.

Goodman, Philip, ed. *The Shavuot Anthology.* Jewish Publication Society of America, 1975.

Goodman, Philip, ed. *The Sukkot and Simhat Torah Anthology.* Jewish Publication Society of America, 1973.

Goodman, Philip, ed. *The Yom Kippur Anthology.* Jewish Publication Society of America, 1971.

Heschel, Abraham J. *The Sabbath.* Farrar, Straus and Giroux, 1975.
The author's magical celebration of the Sabbath and the sanctification of time over space.

Marcus, Audrey F., and Zwerin, Raymond A. *But This Night Is Different.* Union of American Hebrew Congregations, 1981.
Beautiful, sensitive portrayal of *Pesach.* For ages six to eight.

Marcus, Audrey F., and Zwerin, Raymond A. *A Purim Album.* Union of American Hebrew Congregations, 1981.

A charming book about *Purim* for young children. For ages six to eight.

Marcus, Audrey F., and Zwerin, Raymond A. *Shabbat Can Be.* Union of American Hebrew Congregations, 1979.

The warm feelings and images of *Shabbat* familiar to a small child are evoked in the simple text and lovely illustrations. For ages six to eight.

Millgram, Abraham. *Sabbath: The Day of Delight.* Jewish Publication Society of America, 1944.

An anthology of materials about the Sabbath, its observance, art, poetry, music, literature, etc.

Schauss, Hayyim. *The Jewish Festivals: History and Observance.* Schocken, 1973.

Details the colorful story of the Jewish festivals and their development, their origin and background, their rich symbolism, ritual practices, and use of ceremonial objects.

A Shabbat Manual. Central Conference of American Rabbis, 1972.

A practical guide to the observance of *Shabbat,* including home services, *Shabbat* songs, selected readings, and a catalogue of the weekly Torah and *haftarah* portions. A tape of blessings and *Shabbat* songs can be ordered with the manual.

HOLOCAUST

Dawidowicz, Lucy S. *The War Against the Jews 1933–1945.* Bantam, 1976.

A major study of the Holocaust. Intensively researched, comprehensive, and authoritative.

Frank, Anne. *Anne Frank: The Diary of a Young Girl.* Revised edition. Doubleday, 1967.

The remarkable, timeless diary of a young girl, describing the changes wrought upon eight people hiding from the Nazis for two years during the occupation of Holland.

Friedlander, Albert H., ed. *Out of the Whirlwind: A Reader of Holocaust Literature.* Schocken, 1976. Paperback.

A thorough and fascinating collection of writings, music, and art about the Holocaust. Includes selections by Elie Wiesel, Anne Frank, Leo Baeck, and Abraham J. Heschel.

Hersey, John. *The Wall.* Modern Library, 1967.
 A powerful work of historical fiction written in diary form about life in the Warsaw Ghetto during the Nazi occupation.

Morse, Arthur D. *While Six Million Died: Chronicle of American Apathy.* Hart, 1975.
 The author builds a convincing case of US governmental indifference and national apathy in the face of the Holocaust. A significant and powerful report.

Rabinowitz, Dorothy. *New Lives: Survivors of the Holocaust Living in America.* Avon, 1977.
 The survivors themselves tell of individual reactions to liberation, arrival in America, starting new jobs and homes and families, and finding their place in a world that did not understand the nightmare from which they had emerged.

Schwarz-Bart, André. *The Last of the Just.* Translated from the French by Stephen Becker. Bantam, 1973.
 Memorable novel about the Holocaust, using the theme of the thirty-six just souls through whose merit the world continues to exist.

Shabbetai, K. *As Sheep to the Slaughter? The Myth of Cowardice.* World Association of the Bergen-Belsen Survivors Associations, 1963.
 Deals with the misconception that Jews went to their deaths without offering resistance.

Spiritual Resistance: Art from the Concentration Camps, 1940–1945. Union of American Hebrew Congregations, 1981.
 The 111 color and black and white reproductions reveal the Holocaust as seen by those who witnessed and suffered the terrors of Nazi extermination efforts.

Wiesel, Elie. *Night.* Avon, 1972.
 Powerful, autobiographical account of a young boy's experiences during the Holocaust.

ISRAEL

Hertzberg, Arthur, ed. *The Zionist Idea.* Atheneum, 1959.
 An extensive collection of essays and readings on Zionist ideology.

Sachar, Howard M. *A History of Israel: From the Rise of Zionism to Our Time.* Knopf, 1979.
 Best one-volume history of the modern State of Israel. Meticulously researched and intelligently written.

JEWISH THOUGHT AND PHILOSOPHY

Borowitz, Eugene. *Modern Varieties of Jewish Thought: A Presentation and Interpretation.* Behrman House, 1981.
 A thoughtful presentation and analysis of the philosophies of the major Jewish thinkers of our time. Includes chapters on Hermann Cohen, Leo Baeck, Mordecai Kaplan, Franz Rosenzweig, Martin Buber, Abraham Heschel, and Joseph D. Soleveitchik.

Cohen, Abraham. *Everyman's Talmud.* Schocken, 1975.
 An explanation of the Talmud's history and makeup is followed by summaries of the major teachings by subject.

Guttman, Julius. *Philosophies of Judaism: The History of Jewish Philosophy from Biblical Times to Franz Rosenzweig.* Schocken, 1973.
 Authoritative history of Jewish philosophy, from biblical times through its period of great vitality in the Middle Ages to the turn of this century.

LIFE CYCLE

Bial, Morrison D. *Liberal Judaism at Home.* Union of American Hebrew Congregations, 1971.
 Easy-to-read guide to Jewish life-cycle events and holidays, giving both traditional and Reform approaches.

Bial, Morrison D. *Your Jewish Child.* Union of American Hebrew Congregations, 1978.
 A primer to help parents and parents-to-be create a Jewish home that promotes Jewish identity. Topics covered include simple ritual, naming a baby, prayer, and how to tell your children about God, death, and afterlife.

Feldman, David M. *Marital Relations, Birth Control, and Abortion in Jewish Law.* Schocken, 1974.

Traditional Jewish perspective on marital relations, contraception, and abortion. The author examines these issues through the teachings of the Talmud, codes, commentaries, and rabbinic responsa.

Gittelsohn, Roland B. *Love, Sex, and Marriage: A Jewish View.* Union of American Hebrew Congregations, 1980.

A modern, candid discussion of Jewish sexual ethics. For grade eleven and up.

Goodman, Philip, and Goodman, Hanna, eds. *The Jewish Marriage Anthology.* Jewish Publication Society of America, 1965.

A volume of ancient and modern sources that depict the unique Jewish understanding of marriage.

Green, Alan S. *Sex, God, and the Sabbath: The Mystery of Jewish Marriage.* Temple Emanu-El, 2200 S. Green Road, Cleveland, Ohio 44121, 1979.

The title is somewhat misleading. This is a beautifully written volume on the meaning of marriage in the Jewish tradition.

Lamm, Maurice. *The Jewish Way in Love and Marriage.* Harper and Row, 1980.

A complete treatment of Jewish marriage customs written from an Orthodox perspective.

Lamm, Maurice. *The Jewish Way in Death and Mourning.* Jonathan David, 1969.

A complete treatment of Jewish mourning customs written from an Orthodox perspective.

Maslin, Simeon J., ed. *Gates of Mitzvah.* Central Conference of American Rabbis, 1979.

A guide to Jewish observance, throughout the life cycle, from the Reform point of view. Includes sections on birth, childhood, education, marriage, the Jewish home, *tsedakah,* death and mourning, and *kashrut.* Also contains notes and references for further study.

Reimer, Jack, ed. *Jewish Reflections on Death.* Schocken, 1975.

Sensitively chosen collection of essays that portray the historical development and current status of the Jewish way of death.

Routtenberg, Lilly S. *The Jewish Wedding Book.* Schocken, 1967.
A practical guide to planning a Jewish wedding.

Sandmel, Samuel. *When a Jew and Christian Marry.* Fortress Press, 1977.
Addresses and helps clarify the issues relating to mixed marriage.

Schauss, Hayyim. *The Lifetime of a Jew: Throughout the Ages of Jewish History.* Union of American Hebrew Congregations, 1976.
The rites, ceremonies, and folklore that have attended the life of the Jew.

Seltzer, Sanford. *Jews and Non-Jews: Falling in Love.* Union of American Hebrew Congregations, 1976.
An informal guide to interfaith marriage for the couples, their families, and the rabbis who counsel them.

Weilerstein, Sadie Rose. *Our Baby.* Women's League for Conservative Judaism, 1964.
A baby book written especially to mark the milestones and the celebrations of holidays in the life of the Jewish child.

LITURGY

Bronstein, Herbert, ed. *A Passover Haggadah.* Central Conference of American Rabbis, 1974.
New *haggadah* of the Reform movement. Contains twenty original watercolors, the complete Passover home service, and an extensive song section musically annotated.

Glatzer, Nahum N., ed. *Language of Faith: A Selection from the Most Expressive Jewish Prayers.* Schocken, 1974.
Prayers from ancient and modern times on such subjects as the Creation, the presence of God, thanksgiving, the cycle of life, Sabbath, and peace.

Hoffman, Lawrence, ed. *Gates of Understanding.* Central Conference of American Rabbis, 1977.
Companion volume to *Gates of Prayer,* giving sources for all of the prayers, meditations, and songs. Chapters on the language and origin of prayer, the Reform liturgy, music in Jewish worship, the role of God, and the structure of the prayer book

Millgram, Abraham E. *Jewish Worship.* Jewish Publication Society of America, 1971.

Surveys the origins, development, and contemporary significance of Jewish liturgy. The author explains all major aspects of Jewish worship and discusses related theological issues as well.

Petuchowski, Jakob J., ed. *Understanding Jewish Prayer.* Ktav, 1972.

The first part deals with the dynamics of Jewish worship from the biblical period through modern times. It discusses such problems as the concept of prayer as "obligation," the place of the Hebrew language in Jewish worship, and the modern challenges to prayer. The second half of the book consists of an anthology of essays on Jewish prayer contributed by outstanding Jewish scholars.

Stern, Chaim, ed. *Gates of the House.* Central Conference of American Rabbis, 1976.

Home prayer book containing services for special occasions in life and scores of meditations for *Shabbat,* festivals, and other traditional occasions.

Stern, Chaim, ed. *Gates of Prayer: The New Union Prayerbook.* Central Conference of American Rabbis, 1975.

Standard liturgical work of the Reform movement. Contains services for weekdays, Sabbaths, and festivals, as well as for Israel Independence Day, Holocaust Remembrance Day, and *Tishah Be'av.* Also contains special readings, meditations, and forty pages of songs complete with transliterations.

Stern, Chaim, ed. *Gates of Repentance.* Central Conference of American Rabbis, 1978.

Prayer book of the Reform movement for the Days of Awe. Contains services, readings, meditations, and songs for *Rosh Hashanah* and *Yom Kippur.* Companion volume to *Gates of Prayer.*

JOURNAL

(Use loose sheets for all "Journal" entries as these will be collected regularly by the instructor and returned with comments.)

BEGINNINGS

Resource Sheet 1

GLOSSARY

(Throughout, in all "Glossaries" fill in the definitions as the terms listed are discussed.)

Berachah (pl. *Berachot*)—

Shehecheyanu—

Resource Sheet 2

BLESSINGS FOR VARIOUS OCCASIONS

Over pastry:

בָּרוּךְ אַתָּה, יְיָ אֱלֹהֵינוּ, מֶלֶךְ הָעוֹלָם, בּוֹרֵא מִינֵי מְזוֹנוֹת.

Baruch Atah Adonai Elohenu Melech ha'olam Borei minei mezonot.
Blessed is the Lord our God, Ruler of the universe, Creator of many kinds of food.

Over food other than bread, fruits, or vegetables, and over liquids other than wine:

בָּרוּךְ אַתָּה, יְיָ אֱלֹהֵינוּ, מֶלֶךְ הָעוֹלָם, שֶׁהַכֹּל נִהְיֶה בִּדְבָרוֹ.

Baruch Aιah Adonai Elohenu Melech ha'olam shehakol niheyeh bidevaro.
Blessed is the Lord our God, Ruler of the universe, by whose word all things come into being.

Over fruits that grow on trees:

בָּרוּךְ אַתָּה, יְיָ אֱלֹהֵינוּ, מֶלֶךְ הָעוֹלָם, בּוֹרֵא פְּרִי הָעֵץ.

Baruch Atah Adonai Elohenu Melech ha'olam Borei peri ha'etz.
Blessed is the Lord our God, Ruler of the universe, Creator of the fruit of the tree.

On seeing lightning or other natural wonders:

בָּרוּךְ אַתָּה, יְיָ אֱלֹהֵינוּ, מֶלֶךְ הָעוֹלָם, עֹשֶׂה מַעֲשֵׂה בְּרֵאשִׁית.

Baruch Atah Adonai Elohenu Melech ha'olam oseh ma'aseh vereshit.
Blessed is the Lord our God, Ruler of the universe, the Source of creative power.

On seeing the ocean:

בָּרוּךְ אַתָּה, יְיָ אֱלֹהֵינוּ, מֶלֶךְ הָעוֹלָם, שֶׁעָשָׂה אֶת הַיָּם הַגָּדוֹל.

Baruch Atah Adonai Elohenu Melech ha'olam she'asah et hayam hagadol.
Blessed is the Lord our God, Ruler of the universe, Maker of the great sea.

Upon recovery from serious illness or upon escape from danger:

בָּרוּךְ אַתָּה, יְיָ אֱלֹהֵינוּ, מֶלֶךְ הָעוֹלָם, שֶׁגְּמָלַנִי כָּל־טוֹב.

Baruch Atah Adonai Elohenu Melech ha'olam shegemalani kol tov.
Blessed is the Lord our God, Ruler of the universe, who bestows great goodness upon me.

Stern, Chaim, ed. *Gates of the House.* New York: Central Conference of American Rabbis, 1976.

Resource Sheet 3

SHEHECHEYANU

בָּרוּךְ אַתָּה, יְיָ אֱלֹהֵינוּ, מֶלֶךְ הָעוֹלָם, שֶׁהֶחֱיָנוּ וְקִיְּמָנוּ וְהִגִּיעָנוּ לַזְּמַן הַזֶּה.

Baruch Atah Adonai Elohenu Melech ha'olam shehecheyanu vekiyemanu vehigianu lazeman hazeh.

Blessed is the Lord our God, Ruler of the universe, for giving us life, for sustaining us, and for enabling us to reach this season.

Stern, Chaim, ed. *Gates of the House.* New York: Central Conference of American Rabbis, 1976.

BIRTH

Resource Sheet 4

GLOSSARY

Berit Milah—

Mohel—

Kvatter, Kvatterin—

Sandak—

Seudat Mitzvah—

Mi Sheberach—

Berit Hachayim—

Pidyon Haben/Habat—

Kiddush Pe'ter Rechem—

Ken Ayin Hara (Kinna Hurra)—

Resource Sheet 5

THE COVENANT OF MILAH

This ritual is conducted on the eighth day.

Baruch haba. בָּרוּךְ הַבָּא.
May he who comes be blessed.

The rite of circumcision has been enjoined upon us as a sign of our covenant with God, as it is written: And God said to Abraham: You shall keep My covenant, you and your children after you. He who is eight days old shall be circumcised, every male throughout your generations.

We recall the prophetic promise that one day the sign of our covenant with God will be imprinted upon our hearts and the hearts of our children, as well as upon our flesh, so that we may rise to the selfless love of God and therein find life.

May we, like our father Abraham, obey the commandment of God: Walk before Me and reach for perfection.

A parent:
Joyfully do we present our son for the covenant of circumcision.

וַיָּקֶם עֵדוּת בְּיַעֲקֹב, וְתוֹרָה שָׂם בְּיִשְׂרָאֵל, אֲשֶׁר צִוָּה אֶת־אֲבוֹתֵינוּ לְהוֹדִיעָם לִבְנֵיהֶם; לְמַעַן יֵדְעוּ דוֹר אַחֲרוֹן בָּנִים יִוָּלֵדוּ.

Vayakem edut beya'akov vetorah sam beyisrael asher tsivah et avotenu lehodiam livenehem; lema'an yedu dor acharon banim yivaledu.
Lord, You established a testimony in Jacob, You set a Teaching in Israel, commanding our ancestors to make them known to their children; that the generations to come—children yet unborn—might know them.

זָכַר לְעוֹלָם בְּרִיתוֹ, דָּבָר צִוָּה לְאֶלֶף דּוֹר: אֲשֶׁר כָּרַת אֶת־אַבְרָהָם, וּשְׁבוּעָתוֹ לְיִשְׂחָק, וַיַּעֲמִידֶהָ לְיַעֲקֹב לְחֹק, לְיִשְׂרָאֵל בְּרִית עוֹלָם.

Zachar le'olam berito davar tsivah le'elef dor: asher karat et Avraham ushevuato leyischak vaya'amide'ah leya'akov lechok leyisrael berit olam.

You are for ever mindful of Your covenant, the word You commanded for a thousand generations: the covenant You made with Abraham; Your sworn promise to Isaac; the commitment You made to Jacob, Your everlasting covenant with Israel.

הוֹדוּ לַיְיָ כִּי־טוֹב, כִּי לְעוֹלָם חַסְדּוֹ.

Hodu ladonai ki tov ki le'olam chasdo.

O give thanks to the Lord, who is good, whose love is everlasting.

Mohel or a parent:

בָּרוּךְ אַתָּה, יְיָ אֱלֹהֵינוּ, מֶלֶךְ הָעוֹלָם, אֲשֶׁר קִדְּשָׁנוּ בְּמִצְוֹתָיו
וְצִוָּנוּ עַל הַמִּילָה.

Baruch Atah Adonai Elohenu Melech ha'olam asher kideshanu be-mitsvotav vetsivanu al hamilah.

Blessed is the Lord our God, Ruler of the universe, by whose *mitzvot* we are hallowed, who has given us the *mitzvah* of circumcision.

(The circumcision is performed.)

A parent:

בָּרוּךְ אַתָּה, יְיָ אֱלֹהֵינוּ, מֶלֶךְ הָעוֹלָם, אֲשֶׁר קִדְּשָׁנוּ בְּמִצְוֹתָיו
וְצִוָּנוּ לְהַכְנִיסוֹ בִּבְרִיתוֹ שֶׁל אַבְרָהָם אָבִינוּ.

Baruch Atah Adonai Elohenu Melech ha'olam asher kideshanu be-mitsvotav vetsivanu lehachniso biverito shel Avraham avinu.

Blessed is the Lord our God, Ruler of the universe, by whose *mitzvot* we are hallowed, who commands us to bring our sons into the covenant of Abraham.

Mohel or leader:

בָּרוּךְ אַתָּה, יְיָ אֱלֹהֵינוּ, מֶלֶךְ הָעוֹלָם, בּוֹרֵא פְּרִי הַגָּפֶן.

Baruch Atah Adonai Elohenu Melech ha'olam Borei peri hagafen.

Blessed is the Lord our God, Ruler of the universe, Creator of the fruit of the vine.

אֱלֹהֵינוּ וֵאלֹהֵי אֲבוֹתֵינוּ, קַיֵּם אֶת־הַיֶּלֶד הַזֶּה לְאָבִיו וּלְאִמּוֹ, וְיִקָּרֵא שְׁמוֹ בְּיִשְׂרָאֵל . . . יִשְׂמַח הָאָב בְּיוֹצֵא חֲלָצָיו וְתָגֵל אִמּוֹ בִּפְרִי בִטְנָהּ. זֶה הַקָּטָן גָּדוֹל יִהְיֶה. כְּשֵׁם שֶׁנִּכְנַס לַבְּרִית כֵּן יִכָּנֵס לְתוֹרָה, לְחֻפָּה, וּלְמַעֲשִׂים טוֹבִים.

Elohenu velohei avotenu kayem et hayeled hazeh le'aviv ule'imo veyikare shemo beyisrael . . . yismach ha'av beyotse chalatsav vetagel imo bifri vitenah. Zeh hakatan gadol yiheyeh. Keshem shenichnas laberit ken yikanes letorah lechupah ulema'asim tovim.

Our God and God of our people, sustain this child, and let him be known in the House of Israel as. . . . May he bring much joy to his parents in the months and years to come. As he has entered into the covenant of Abraham, so may he enter into the study of Torah, the blessing of marriage, and the practice of goodness.

מִי שֶׁבֵּרַךְ אֲבוֹתֵינוּ אַבְרָהָם, יִצְחָק, וְיַעֲקֹב, הוּא יְבָרֵךְ אֶת־הַיֶּלֶד הָרַךְ הַנִּמּוֹל וִירַפֵּא אוֹתוֹ רְפוּאָה שְׁלֵמָה. וְיִזְכּוּ אֲבוֹתָיו לְגַדְּלוֹ לְחַנְּכוֹ וּלְחַכְּמוֹ. וְיִהְיוּ יָדָיו וְלִבּוֹ לְאֵל אֱמוּנָה, וְנֹאמַר: אָמֵן.

Mi sheberach avotenu Avraham Yitschak veya'akov hu yevarech et hayeled harach hanimol virape oto refu'ah shelemah. Veyizeku avotav legadelo lechanecho ulechakemo. Veyiheyu yadav velibo le'el emunah venomar: Amen.

May the One who blessed our fathers, Abraham, Isaac, and Jacob, bless this child and keep him from all harm. May his parents rear him to dedicate his life in faithfulness to God, his heart receptive always to Torah and *mitzvot.* Then shall he bring blessing to his parents, his people, and all the world.

יְבָרֶכְךָ יְיָ וְיִשְׁמְרֶךָ,
יָאֵר יְיָ פָּנָיו אֵלֶיךָ וִיחֻנֶּךָּ,
יִשָּׂא יְיָ פָּנָיו אֵלֶיךָ וְיָשֵׂם לְךָ שָׁלוֹם.

Yevarechecha Adonai veyishmerecha
Ya'er Adonai panav elecha vichuneka
Yisa Adonai panav elecha veyasem lecha shalom.
The Lord bless you and keep you

The Lord look kindly upon you and be gracious to you
The Lord bestow favor upon you and give you peace, Amen.

The service might conclude with a reading in the form of an alphabetical acrostic of the child's name, selected from Psalm 119 or other scriptural verses.

Stern, Chaim, ed. *Gates of the House.* New York: Central Conference of American Rabbis, 1976.

Resource Sheet 6

THE COVENANT OF LIFE

This ritual is conducted on the eighth day.

Beruchah haba'ah.
May she who comes be blessed.

בְּרוּכָה הַבָּאָה.

Reverence for life has been enjoined upon us as a fulfillment of our covenant with God, as it is written: And God said to Israel: Choose life, that you and your descendants may live. The birth of a daughter brings us joy and hope, and the courage to reaffirm our enduring covenant with life and its Creator.

The mother kindles a light and takes her daughter:
    Joyfully I bring my daughter into the covenant of Israel: covenant with God, with Torah, and with life.

בָּרוּךְ אַתָּה, יְיָ אֱלֹהֵינוּ, מֶלֶךְ הָעוֹלָם, אֲשֶׁר קִדְּשָׁנוּ בְּמִצְוֹתָיו וְצִוָּנוּ עַל קִדּוּשׁ הַחַיִּים.

Baruch Atah Adonai Elohenu Melech ha'olam asher kideshanu be-mitsvotav vetsivanu al kidush hachayim.
Blessed is the Lord our God, Ruler of the universe, by whose *mitzvot* we are hallowed, who commands us to sanctify life.

The father kindles a light and takes his daughter:

אֲנִי יְיָ, וְאֶתֶּנְךָ לִבְרִית עָם, לְאוֹר גּוֹיִם.

Ani Adonai ve'etenecha liverit am le'or goyim.
I, the Lord, have made you a covenant people, a light to the nations.

כִּי נֵר מִצְוָה וְתוֹרָה אוֹר.

Ki ner mitzvah vetorah or.
For the *mitzvah* is a lamp and the Torah a light.

בָּרוּךְ אַתָּה, יְיָ, הַמֵּאִיר לָעוֹלָם כֻּלּוֹ בִּכְבוֹדוֹ.

Baruch Atah Adonai hame'ir la'olam kulo bichevodo.
Blessed is the Lord, whose presence gives light to all the world.

Both parents say:

בָּרוּךְ אַתָּה, יְיָ אֱלֹהֵינוּ, מֶלֶךְ הָעוֹלָם, שֶׁהֶחֱיָנוּ וְקִיְּמָנוּ וְהִגִּיעָנוּ לַזְּמַן הַזֶּה.

Baruch Atah Adonai Elohenu Melech ha'olam shehecheyanu vekiyemanu vehigianu lazeman hazeh.

Blessed is the Lord our God, Ruler of the universe, for giving us life, for sustaining us, and for enabling us to reach this day of joy.

זֶה הַיּוֹם עָשָׂה יְיָ; נָגִילָה וְנִשְׂמְחָה בוֹ!

Zeh hayom asah Adonai; nagilah venismechah vo!

This is the day the Lord has made; let us rejoice and be glad in it!

וַיָּקֶם עֵדוּת בְּיַעֲקֹב, וְתוֹרָה שָׂם בְּיִשְׂרָאֵל, אֲשֶׁר צִוָּה אֶת־אֲבוֹתֵינוּ לְהוֹדִיעָם לִבְנֵיהֶם; לְמַעַן יֵדְעוּ דוֹר אַחֲרוֹן בָּנִים יִוָּלֵדוּ.

Vayakem edut beya'akov vetorah sam beyisrael asher tsivah et avotenu lehodiam livenehem; lema'an yedu dor acharon banim yivaledu.

Lord, You established a testimony among us, You set a Teaching in Israel, commanding our ancestors to make them known to their children; that the generations to come—children yet unborn—might know them.

זָכַר לְעוֹלָם בְּרִיתוֹ, דָּבָר צִוָּה לְאֶלֶף דּוֹר: אֲשֶׁר כָּרַת אֶת־אַבְרָהָם, וּשְׁבוּעָתוֹ לְיִשְׂחָק, וַיַּעֲמִידֶהָ לְיַעֲקֹב לְחֹק, לְיִשְׂרָאֵל בְּרִית עוֹלָם.

Zachar le'olam berito davar tsivah le'elef dor: asher karat et Avraham ushevuato leyischak vaya'amide'ah leya'akov lechok leyisrael berit olam.

You are for ever mindful of Your covenant, the word You commanded for a thousand generations: the covenant You made with the founders. Your sworn promise to their descendants, the commitment You made to our people, Your everlasting covenant with Israel.

הוֹדוּ לַיְיָ כִּי־טוֹב, כִּי לְעוֹלָם חַסְדּוֹ.

Hodu ladonai ki tov ki le'olam chasdo.

O give thanks to the Lord, who is good, whose love is everlasting.

בָּרוּךְ אַתָּה, יְיָ אֱלֹהֵינוּ, מֶלֶךְ הָעוֹלָם, בּוֹרֵא פְּרִי הַגָּפֶן.

Baruch Atah Adonai Elohenu Melech ha'olam Borei peri hagafen.

Blessed is the Lord our God, Ruler of the universe, Creator of the fruit of the vine.

אֱלֹהֵינוּ וֵאלֹהֵי אִמּוֹתֵינוּ, קַיֵּם אֶת־הַיַּלְדָּה הַזֹּאת לְאָבִיהָ
וּלְאִמָּהּ, וְיִקָּרֵא שְׁמָהּ בְּיִשְׂרָאֵל . . . יִשְׂמַח הָאָב בְּיוֹצֵאת
חֲלָצָיו וְתָגֵל אִמָּהּ בִּפְרִי בִטְנָהּ. זֹאת הַקְּטַנָּה גְּדוֹלָה תִּהְיֶה.
כְּשֵׁם שֶׁנִּכְנְסָה לַבְּרִית כֵּן תִּכָּנֵס לַתּוֹרָה, לְחֻפָּה, וּלְמַעֲשִׂים
טוֹבִים.

Elohenu velohei imotenu kayem et hayaldah hazot le'aviah ule'imah
veyikare shemah beyisrael . . . yismach ha'av beyotset chalatsav vetagel
imah bifri vitenah. Zot haketanah gedolah tiheyeh. Keshem shenich-
nesah laberit ken tikanes letorah lechupah ulema'asim tovim.

Our God, God of all generations, sustain this child, and let her be
known in the House of Israel as. . . . May she bring much joy to her
parents in the months and years to come. As she has entered into the
covenant of life, so may she enter into the study of Torah, the
blessing of marriage, and the practice of goodness.

מִי שֶׁבֵּרַךְ אִמּוֹתֵינוּ שָׂרָה, רִבְקָה, רָחֵל, וְלֵאָה, הוּא יְבָרֵךְ
אֶת־הַיַּלְדָּה הָרַכָּה וְיִשְׁמְרֶהָ מִכָּל־צָרָה וְצוּקָה. וְיִזְכּוּ הוֹרֶיהָ
לְגַדְּלָהּ לְחַנְּכָהּ וּלְחַכְּמָהּ. וְיִהְיוּ יָדֶיהָ וְלִבָּהּ לְאֵל אֱמוּנָה,
וְנֹאמַר: אָמֵן.

Mi sheberach imotenu Sarah Rivkah Ruchel veleah hu yevarech et
hayaldah harukah veyishmere'ah mikol tsarah vetsukah. Veyizeku
hore'ah legadelah lechanechah ulechakemah. Veyiheyu yade'ah veli-
bah le'el emunah venomar: Amen.

May the One who blessed our mothers, Sarah, Rebekah, Leah, and
Rachel, bless this child and keep her from all harm. May her parents
rear her to dedicate her life in faithfulness to God, her heart receptive
always to Torah and *mitzvot.* Then shall she bring blessing to her
parents, her people, and all the world.

יְבָרֶכְךָ יְיָ וְיִשְׁמְרֶךָ,
יָאֵר יְיָ פָּנָיו אֵלֶיךָ וִיחֻנֶּךָּ,
יִשָּׂא יְיָ פָּנָיו אֵלֶיךָ וְיָשֵׂם לְךָ שָׁלוֹם.

Yevarechecha Adonai veyishmerecha
Ya'er Adonai panav elecha vichuneka
Yisa Adonai panav elecha veyasem lecha shalom.

The Lord bless you and keep you
The Lord look kindly upon you and be gracious to you
The Lord bestow favor upon you and give you peace. Amen.

Stern, Chaim, ed. *Gates of the House.* New York: Central Conference of American Rabbis, 1976.

For further information on *Berit Milah* and *Berit Hachayim,* see *The Jewish Home,* Book 7; for information on *Pidyon Haben,* see *The Jewish Home,* Book 8.

Resource Sheet 7

CCAR STATEMENTS ON BIRTH CONTROL

1. We approve the Cummins-Vail Bill. (1926, p.109)
2. We urge the recognition of the importance of the control of parenthood as one of the methods of coping with social problems. (1929, p.86)
3. We urge recognition of the importance of intelligent birth regulation. We are aware of the many serious evils caused by lack of birth control. (1930, p.78, report)
4. Reaffirms 1930 report and goes on record as favoring the inclusion of Planned Parenthood services in hospitals and other agencies where this service should be given and urges that the Board of Directors of health and welfare agencies permit their professional staff members to make maximum use of these services as a community health resource. (1947, pp.219–220)

Stevens, Elliot, and Glaser, Simeon, eds. *Resolutions of the Central Conference.* Revised edition. New York: Central Conference of American Rabbis, 1975.

Reform Judaism respects the right of parents to determine how many children they should have. In considering family size, however, parents should be aware of the tragic decimation of our people during the Holocaust and of the threats of annihilation that have pursued the Jewish people through history. Thus, while Reform Judaism approves of the practice of birth control, couples are encouraged to consider the matter of family size carefully and with due regard to the problem of Jewish survival.

Maslin, Simeon J., ed. *Gates of Mitzvah.* New York: Central Conference of American Rabbis, 1979.

Resource Sheet 8

CCAR STATEMENTS ON ABORTION

The Central Conference of American Rabbis considers as religiously valid and humane such new legislation that recognizes the preservation of a mother's emotional health to be as important as her physical well-being; and properly considers the danger of anticipated physical or mental damage; and permits abortion in pregnancies resulting from sexual crime including rape, statutory rape, and incest.

We strongly urge the broad liberalization of abortion laws in the various states and call upon our members to work toward this end. (1967, p.103)

Stevens, Elliot, and Glaser, Simeon, eds. *Resolutions of the Central Conference.* Revised edition. New York: Central Conference of American Rabbis, 1975.

In keeping with the fundamental principle of the sanctity of life, Judaism has since ancient times allowed and even prescribed abortion in cases where the life or health of the mother is in danger. In keeping with this tradition, and recognizing that one's emotional health is as important as one's physical health, Reform Judaism affirms the right of a woman, after due regard to the sanctity of life and in accordance with the principles of Jewish morality, to determine whether or not she can continue a pregnancy to term. Abortion may be medically indicated in cases where genetic disease or malformation of the fetus is probable. In all such cases the mother and father should consult with their rabbi.

Maslin, Simeon J., ed. *Gates of Mitzvah.* New York: Central Conference of American Rabbis, 1979.

WHAT IS YOUR NAME?

by Harold Friedman

Once, when I was a little boy, I got lost in the May Company—in the handkerchief department.

My mother told me to stay close to her while she shopped for presents. It was Chanukah time, I remember, and it was raining outside. I let go of my mother's skirt and went to the big front door. I stuck my nose against the door and watched the raindrops sliding down the glass. When I turned around, my mother was gone. And I was lost.

The salesladies were very nice—but I didn't know any of them.

The manager came over and he was nice, too—but I didn't know him either.

A whole crowd of people came around—they told me not to worry—but I didn't know any of them either.

They were all big people, big people I didn't know, and I was very little. I was frightened and I began to cry.

Then the manager bent down and took my hand and he said, "Little boy, what is your name?"

"Dan Segal," I said.

"My name is Dan Segal," I said. And something wonderful happened. "My name is Dan Segal," I told him, and I stopped crying. I didn't feel a bit like crying any more, I felt warm and good inside. I felt good because I knew my name, and I could tell it. I could say my name and everybody would know who I was. There was nothing more to worry about then; it would be easy to get me back to my mother; everything was all right.

I knew my name, so I wasn't frightened any more.

I knew my name, so I wasn't lost any more.

I was somebody—because I knew my name.

Once, when I was a little boy, I got lost in the May Company. But the other day I saw a boy get lost right in our classroom in public school. He knew his name all right—Jimmy Samuels. He even knew his address. But he was lost just the same, as lost as I was in the May

Company. At first I didn't understand—well, I'd like to tell you about it.

We were studying about America, I guess. And Miss Statler, that's our teacher, went around the room asking the children, and they stood up and told about the countries their parents or grandparents or great-grandparents had come from, and what their people had done to help build up America and make it a good place to live in, and all interesting things about them. The boy next to me told some interesting things about Holland, and the girl on the other side knew some good things about Ireland, and she even sang an Irish lullaby for us. It was beautiful. And then Miss Statler called on Jimmy Samuels, and Jimmy just sat there.

Miss Statler looked at him; she said, "Jimmy, surely you know something interesting to tell; you're Jewish, aren't you?"

I looked at Jimmy and right away I knew he felt just the way I did that day at the May Company. I could just see it on his face. He got all red, and his eyes filled up, and he looked this way and that just like I did when I was scared and looking for my mother. I couldn't understand why he looked so funny, and then Miss Statler went on and she called on me.

So I stood up and said a few things. I guess I started with how the word Jewish comes from Judah, and he was one of the sons of Jacob, and that name sticks in all Jewish history. The kids were listening all right, and Miss Statler nodded to me, so I told a little more of the things I learned in the synagogue—some of the things the Jewish people had done, like getting rid of idols, and fighting to be free from the Egyptians and the Greeks and all the other bad people, and working for the Ten Commandments, and all the fine holidays, and how Sukot was much like Thanksgiving, and our country was believing in the ideas of the Hebrew Bible, and I guess maybe something about great men in America who are Jews.

I probably talked too long but I learned quite a bit in synagogue —and then, all of a sudden, when I sat down, I had a funny feeling. I felt just the way I did when I remembered my name in the May Company and said it out clear and loud. I felt good inside, all warm and comfortable. I felt just as if I knew my name.

So now I wonder if maybe a person can get lost even if he knows his name and his address perfectly well—if there isn't more than one kind of a name that goes with a person. Seems as if there's a name your family calls you—like Jimmy or Dan.

And maybe there's another kind of name that you call yourself

—inside—the kind of a name you get from learning something about yourself and your people, and who you are and where you came from, and what's good and useful about you so you feel as good as the next person and understand that they are as good as you. My name is Jewish, that inside name—and I guess I'm lucky, I know that inside name, too.

It's the sort of a name Jimmy Samuels doesn't know because he never comes to synagogue, and I guess maybe his parents don't care if he looks lost and his face gets red and he looks as if he's going to cry. I wish they would, though. Because you have no idea what a good feeling it is to know your name. To stand up and say it out loud and strong when somebody asks you.

You can't be frightened—when you know your name.

You can't get lost—when you know your name.

You're somebody—when you know your name.

Eisenberg, Azriel, ed. *The Bar Mitzvah Treasury.* New York: Behrman House, Inc., 1952.

CHANUKAH

Resource Sheet 10

GLOSSARY

Chanukah—

Chanukat Habayit—

Menorah—

Chanukiah—

Gelt—

Dreidel—

Nes Gadol Hayah Sham—

Latke—

Sufganiyot—

THE HISTORICAL BACKGROUND OF CHANUKAH

by Victoria Kelman

Alexander the Great conquered the area known as Palestine in 331 B.C.E. and Judea was absorbed into the Greek empire, along with most of that part of the world. Following Alexander's death in 323 B.C.E., his empire was divided between his generals, and Palestine lay between two newly-created monarchies—that of Ptolemy of Egypt and that of Seleucid of Syria. Palestine was desired by both and was at the core of dispute between the two, changing hands several times for at least 100 years after Alexander's death.

At first, Judea was part of Egypt. The Ptolemies left the Jews to govern themselves. Judea was granted the status of a Temple state, which meant that the high priest served as both religious and political leader of his country.

In the wake of Alexander's conquest, Greek cultural influence spread in all the lands of his conquest. This was not surprising. The Greek culture was the first culture which extended beyond national borders. To that point in history, a person's culture could only be the one into which he was born. But Greek culture was unique in that it was attainable by education. It was immensely attractive and began to take hold everywhere. Judea was no exception. Although Greek influence filtered in as a result of contacts with armies, traders, and foreign dignitaries, it came predominantly by way of contact with Jews in the Diaspora. In cities like Alexandria, capital of Ptolemaic Egypt, Jews spoke Greek, dedicated two synagogues to Ptolemy, and began to refer to God by Zeus's epithet, "God Most High." They retained observance of the Torah (which had to be translated into Greek which had become their native tongue).

As the tide of Greek influence swelled, Antiochus (a Seleucid) drove Ptolemy V out of Judea and annexed it to the Seleucid (Syrian) empire in 198 B.C.E. Antiochus III retained Jerusalem as a Temple state, decreed a tax relief, and promised the Jews freedom to enjoy their traditional way of life.

By the time Antiochus IV inherited the throne from his father (175 B.C.E.), Hellenism was already on the rise in Judea. Jewish citizens who considered themselves modern and advanced had begun to adopt Hellenistic culture. Hellenism as used here means "in the Greek fashion." It refers to the much-diluted Greek culture more typical of second-century Antioch (Syrian capital) than of fifth-century Athens. The word Hellenizers will be used to indicate those who worked to spread Hellenism. It was not long before gymnasia and Greek culture arrived in Jerusalem. The importance of the gymnasium should not be overlooked. It was far more than a place of physical education. In fact it was *the* primary Greek educational center for men. In the gymnasium, naked sports and lectures by the philosophers were carried on in proximity. A youth movement involving young men in cultural and physical education as well as in premilitary training was attached to each gymnasium. All the activities which took place there were considered to be under the hospitality and protection of the Greek gods. Jews strove to be Greek fully: speaking Greek, wearing the Greek toga, translating their names into Greek, participating in the naked sports of gymnasia competition (in some cases having undergone painful operations to hide the evidence of circumcision), and playing in games to honor the Greek gods. They forsook traditional Jewish study to pursue politics, philosophy, commerce, drama, and physical culture.

Jason, the high priest at this time, was one of the leaders of the Hellenizers. He had become high priest by promising Antiochus extra revenues in return for the "privilege" of building a gymnasium on the slopes of the Temple hill. As political and religious leader, this "puppet" of Antiochus was in a unique position to foster political closeness with Syria which in turn fostered the growth of Hellenism in Judea.

Within Judea, there was constant squabbling over the conflicting claims to the high priesthood, between groups preferring rule by Egypt to rule by Syria, and between Hellenists and anti-Hellenists.

In addition, Antiochus was facing problems within his large and varied empire and pressure from Rome and Ptolemy from without. It seemed to him that the solution lay in unification of his empire into a peaceful and cohesive unit. He decided that he needed to create a balance between Greek and Oriental populations. He did this by two policies: actually moving populations from one area to another and proclaiming a unifying religion to which all subjects were to adhere. All subjects were to worship Zeus of whom he was to be considered the earthly manifestation. He took on the name Epiphanes (God made manifest) to underline this. This religious policy offered Jews (and all others in the empire) the opportunity to become equals. The Hellenizers rejoiced!

But the majority of Jews failed to embrace this religion of their own free will. From our various sources, it seems most likely that Antiochus had been misled by the new High Priest Menelaus (he had become high priest by offering Antiochus more money than Jason could come up with) who told him that all the Jews would be delighted to go along with this new religion. His predictions were not borne out. In Antiochus's eyes, the opposition to the ruling party, as represented by the high priest, was tantamount to rebellion, and rebellion near the borders of Egypt constituted a danger to the security of his empire. Antiochus feared that this expression of nationalism (which is how he viewed the adherence to Torah) would threaten the peace he so desperately sought. He concluded that by abolishing the Torah, source of the Jews' separatism, he would achieve his dual ends of peace within Judea along with its integration into the rest of his empire.

Scholars disagree as to whether the decrees known to history as "the persecutions of Antiochus" were creations of Antiochus or Menelaus. But, regardless of the idea's originator, it is clear that the two cooperated in the decision to institute the death penalty as punishment for observing the Torah and to force Jews to acknowledge Zeus.

There were Jews who openly defied the king and were martyred. Some tried to avoid participation in pagan rituals without open refusal. Many Jews avoided participation in idolatrous rites by fleeing the cities to live freely (as outlaws) in the wilds of the countryside.

Hoping to force all to adhere to the order of the king, his agents journeyed from city to city to force public adherence to the king's laws. They would set up an altar in the marketplaces, gather all the people together, and require them to worship Zeus and taste the flesh of the offerings.

In the winter of 166 B.C.E., the king's agents arrived in the town of Modin (near Lod on the Jerusalem-Jaffa road). When the first Jew came forward before the altar in order to bow down, Mattathias, a local priest, jumped forward and killed both the man and the king's messenger. He tore down the altar and bid all who would honor God and Torah to follow him.

Mattathias and his five sons fled to the wilderness. There soon gathered around them many others with like concerns who had previously fled to elude breaking Jewish law. They decided to replace passive resistance with active struggle. *The main thrust of their attack was at the Jewish Hellenizers, not at the Syrian Greeks.* This brought Judea to the brink of civil war. Tensions between the two groups of Jews, which had seethed under the surface for years, broke into the open.

For two years this small group, led after Mattathias's death by his third son, Judah, waged guerrilla war on Hellenized Jews, moving into small towns, striking swiftly and moving on.

The main party of Hellenizers living comfortable lives in Jerusalem paid very little attention to the bloodshed in the countryside. The Syrians, considering this to be a small matter of only local importance, also paid no attention.

However, when Judah and his band gained control of the Jerusalem-Jaffa highway (the main road to Jerusalem), he *did* gain the attention of the Syrians for having disrupted communications and control. The Syrians sent their army against Judah but had little success with their phalanx-trained army fighting in rocky hills against the Jewish guerrillas.

Antiochus had very little interest in local Jewish affairs—what these people are or how they worshiped was not of great consequence to him. His treasury was empty and he could not risk any trouble on his border with Ptolemy, so he negotiated a settlement in which he agreed to cancel the ban on observance of Torah and cancel his insistence that all worship Zeus.

The persecutions were ended. But the high priest and his party were still in control of the Temple and there were *mitzvot* which could only be carried out there. This forced Judah to regather his disbanded forces for a sudden attack on Jerusalem in order to wrest control from these Hellenizers. They succeeded in conquering the city. They cleansed the Temple and restored the Temple service. The rededication of the Temple took place on 25 *Kislev* and the celebration continued for eight days. Judah declared this a holiday to be kept for generations to come.

Resource Sheet 12

TALMUD SANHEDRIN 37A: THE COIN MIDRASH

For this reason was man created alone: to teach thee that, whosoever destroys a single soul of Israel, Scripture imputes [guilt] to him as though he had destroyed a complete world; and, whosoever preserves a single soul of Israel, Scripture ascribes [merit] to him as though he had preserved a complete world. Furthermore [he was created alone], for the sake of peace among men, that one might not say to his fellow: "My father was greater than thine," and that the minim might not say: "There are many ruling powers in heaven"; again, to proclaim the greatness of the Holy One, blessed be He; for, if a man strikes many coins from one mold, they all resemble one another, but the supreme King of kings, the Holy One, blessed be He, fashioned every man in the stamp of the first man, and yet not one of them resembles his fellow. Therefore, every single person is obliged to say: "The world was created for my sake."

The Babylonian Talmud. London: The Soncino Press Ltd.

NOT BY MIGHT, NOT BY POWER

words and music by Debbie Friedman

Not by might and not by power
But by spirit alone
Shall all men live in peace.

Not by might and not by power
But by spirit alone
Shall all men live in peace.

The children sing
The children dream
And their tears may fall
But we'll hear them call
And another song will rise
Another song will rise
Another song will rise.

Resource Sheet 14

TALMUD SHABBAT 21B

Our Rabbis taught: The precept of *Chanukah* [demands] one light for a man and his household; the zealous [kindle] a light for each member [of the household]; and the extremely zealous—Bet Shammai maintains: On the first day eight lights are lit and thereafter they are gradually reduced; but Bet Hillel says: On the first day one is lit and thereafter they are progressively increased. Ulla said: In the West [Palestine] two *amoraim*, R. Jose b. Abin and R. Jose b. Zebida, differ therein; one maintains: The reason of Bet Shammai is that it shall correspond to the days still to come and that of Bet Hillel is that it shall correspond to the days that are gone; but another maintains: Bet Shammai's reason is that it shall correspond to the bullocks of the festival, whilst Bet Hillel's reason is that we promote in [matters of] sanctity but do not reduce.

Rabbah b. Bar Hana said: There were two old men in Sidon; one did as Bet Shammai and the other as Bet Hillel: the former gave the reason of his action that it should correspond to the bullocks of the festival, while the latter stated his reason because we promote in [matters of] sanctity but do not reduce.

Our Rabbis taught: It is incumbent to place the *Chanukah* lamp by the door of one's house on the outside; if one dwells in an upper chamber, he places it at the window nearest the street. But in times of danger it is sufficient to place it on the table. Raba said: Another lamp is required for its light to be used, yet if there is a blazing fire it is unnecessary. But, in the case of an important person, even if there is a blazing fire, another lamp is required.

What is [the reason of] *Chanukah?* For our Rabbis taught: On the twenty-fifth of *Kislev* [commence] the days of *Chanukah,* which are eight on which a lamentation for the dead and fasting are forbidden. For, when the Greeks entered the Temple, they defiled all the oils therein and, when the Hasmonean dynasty prevailed against and defeated them, they made search and found only one cruse of oil which lay with the seal of the high priest, but which contained sufficient for one day's lighting only; yet a miracle was wrought

therein and they lit [the lamp] therewith for eight days. The following year these [days] were appointed a festival with [the recital of]
Hallel and thanksgiving.

The Babylonian Talmud. London: The Soncino Press Ltd.

Resource Sheet 15

DECEMBER DILEMMA: THE MENORAH OR THE TREE

by Rabbi Roland B. Gittelsohn

One of the most pathetic spectacles in American Jewish life at this time of the year is the Jew who justifies the observance of Christmas on the ground that it is a secular national holiday with no religious significance. Though it be in a sense cruel to deprive such a person of the reassuring rationalizations, both honesty and Jewish self-respect require that we face Christmas honestly for what it really is. What, then, is the real significance of those seemingly-innocent Christmas customs with which so many of our people delight to adorn their homes?

THE TREE

Like many other ceremonies and symbols of both Judaism and Christianity, the Christmas tree may have originated in pagan life. It was soon given deeply religious significance, however, by Christianity. Its early Christian use was based on a legend that the night Jesus was born all the trees of the forest bloomed and bore fruit, despite the snow and ice which covered them. By more thoughtful and theologically-minded Christians the tree is still meant today to symbolize the resurrection and immortality of Jesus, as well as the wood used for the cross of crucifixion. Grim irony, indeed, that Jews, so many of whose ancestors were persecuted and perished because of their alleged complicity in the crucifixion of Jesus, should now embrace a symbol of that very event!

In 1932 one Christian authority summarized the significance of the Christmas tree in these words—"In quieter moments its real significance may be hinted: For it is a symbol of Christ, as the tree of life who offers freely to all his gifts of light and life and wisdom."

ITS DECORATIONS

Of what religious significance are the decorations used on the Christmas tree? One explanation goes back to Martin Luther whom the stars in the sky reminded one Christmas eve of "him who for us men and for our salvation came down from heaven."

The tinsel seen on Christmas trees is known as "angel's hair." It is meant to recall the heavenly hosts who are supposed to have attended the miraculous birth of the Christian savior.

The apples which were once part of the tree's adornment and the simulated apples more commonly used today are supposed to remind us of the apple which tempted Adam and Eve in Eden. Christian doctrine teaches that from the seeds of that very apple there grew the tree used for the cross on which Jesus met his death.

MISTLETOE AND HOLLY

Surely the inhibition removing mistletoe at least is devoid of religious significance? Must we be deprived of this too?

I'm afraid we must. No better description of the place of mistletoe in the Christian scheme of things can be found than in the words of a popular Christmas hymn:

> *The mistletoe bow at our Christmas board*
> *Shall hang to the honor of Christ our Lord:*
> *For he is the evergreen tree of life. . . .*

And the holly wreath? One Christian spokesman tells us that it represents "the crown of thorns which Christ wore on the cross, the little red berries symbolizing the drops of blood."

LAST REFUGE

A final question remains, the last refuge of the Jew who would cling emotionally to the celebration of Christmas even after being assured intellectually that its religious significance is not for the Jew: "But can't we Jews observe Christmas as a secular occasion without accepting the theology it symbolizes?" Of course we can. That's not the real question. The real question is: "Do we have a moral right to?"

What would be our reaction if any significant number of Christians were to begin celebrating *Yom Kippur,* the holiest day in our religious calendar, as a secular occasion—a day devoid of all sacred significance, a day for unbounded hilarity and exaggerated commercialization? What right have we to expect our devout Christian neighbors to take any more kindly to the dilution of their most sacred day than we would to ours?

This question and the answer implied by its very asking are not imaginary on my part. Sensitive Jews, even if not compelled by an inner integrity and self-respect to celebrate *Chanukah* rather than Christmas, might well heed the advice in *The Churchman,* December 15, 1950:

> Whatever external elements the festivals of *Chanukah* and Christmas . . . may have in common, this fact remains: *Chanukah* is distinctly Jewish and Christmas is as distinctly Christian. . . . This should be remembered to the advantage of the Jew and Christian. . . . If the season of *Chanukah* and Christmas is always to be one of peace and goodwill, let both Jew and Christian remember that they have a right to perpetuate and preserve their particular cultural and religious mores and that any attempts at reckless and superficial assimilation are as stupid as they are bound to be futile.

SHOULD JEWS CELEBRATE CHRISTMAS?

by Rabbi Henry E. Kagan

Q: Since Christmas is now almost as much a national as well as a religious holiday, can't all Americans, regardless of religion, join in the celebration?

A: Christmas is not the Fourth of July or any other secular American holiday and it would be an insult to my Christian friends to regard it as anything but what it is—*the most important Christian holy day.* Since it celebrates the birth of the Christian world's messiah and since Jews do not accept Jesus as messiah, Christmas cannot come within the area of Jewish celebration.

Q: But can it be harmful to have Christmas trees in Jewish homes and for Jewish children to receive Christmas presents?

A: All children have a real need for religious ritual and material symbols of faith. But for Jewish parents to gratify this need by rituals and symbols that are fundamentally "forbidden fruit" to the child is harmful. Christmas belongs to the Christians; it has no place in a Jewish home.

Q: But won't this make Jews feel "different" and left out at Christmas?

A: The wonderful thing about America is that it gives us the right to be different. Jewish children are a minority, they are different religiously. They must learn to face this with pride in their own practices and beliefs. If the parent simply takes away Christmas and puts nothing in its place, the child is being cheated. But this needn't happen; Judaism has its own beautiful holidays, *Chanukah,* for instance, which falls so close to Christmas, and during which it is traditional for Jews to exchange presents. Jewish holidays are what belong to the Jew; if the parents celebrate these days in a meaningful way, the child will have no need to look to another religion.

CLARIFYING CONFUSION

by Dr. Max Nussbaum

There are personal, Jewish, American, and universal holidays which a Jew can legitimately celebrate; and there are others, basically Christian or Moslem holidays, which belong to the sacred repository of other religions and have, therefore, to be left alone by a conscientious Jew.

There is a simple criterion by which to test the legitimacy of holiday celebration. Whenever you can put a holiday into the synagogue, weave it into the tapestry of a service, and watch it fit harmoniously into the mosaic of Judaism—then and then only can a holiday be celebrated in good conscience.

Birthdays and wedding anniversaries, all Jewish holidays in the rhythm of the Jewish calendar, all American holidays—the Fourth of July, Memorial Day, Washington's and Lincoln's birthdays—which stem from the very historical experience of the nation, and all universal holidays—Brotherhood Week, United Nations Month, the secular New Year—can, therefore, and have actually been made a part of the religious service of the synagogue in perfect blending with the idealism of our ancient tradition.

Imagine for a single moment to do the same with Christmas and you will discover at first glance that it doesn't belong to you and you don't belong to it because it stands as a sacred symbol of basic Christianity. And it is as immoral to trespass upon the theological tradition of another religion as it is to help oneself to the accumulated bank account of a neighbor on your block.

A CHALLENGE TO JEWISH PARENTS: WHAT TO DO ABOUT THE CHRISTMAS TREE

by Rabbi Theodore Gordon

In the life of the American child, December is a happy month, for it brings holiday spirit, parties, and presents. To many American Jewish parents, December brings a troublesome problem: whether to pivot these parties and presents about *Chanukah* or to reserve them for the date when the community at large is celebrating its Christmas holiday.

This year, as in other years, many Jewish parents will be greatly distressed by the appeals of their children for Christmas trees and Christmas trimmings. Once again some Jewish parents accede to the pleas of their children, offering any one of a dozen reasons (or rationalizations): To refuse would make the children unhappy, deprive them of something of real charm and beauty, cut them off from celebrating one of America's folk holidays ("the Christmas tree really has no *religious significance*"), give them a sense of "differentness" from their neighbors and playmates, etc.

Those of us for whom Jewish life is meaningful cannot dismiss too lightly the impact of this problem upon a large number of Jewish parents. In Jewish home after home, we have encountered such situations, with children asking for what their playmates have and parents, hopelessly confused in their thinking, proceeding, even with the best of intentions, to scuttle what remains of Jewish value and sentiment in the home.

Since this annually recurring crisis is again at hand, it might be well to examine the problem and clarify a few fundamental points with reference to it.

I

At the very outset it should be made clear that this is a problem of Jewish *parents,* not Jewish children. . . . The same mother who insists upon her child's eating spinach and washing behind the ears is somehow helpless to oppose his whims in the matter of a Christmas tree. The father who through the year is not too concerned with giving his children a full and rich folk experience becomes suddenly worried lest they "miss out on something beautiful and worthwhile."

In the continuous battle of wits between parents and children, the latter are quick to pick out the weak spots in their parents' line and drive through to their own advantage. Most parents actually *invite* the request for a Christmas celebration by their own obvious indecision and by their lack of Jewish convictions and loyalties which children are quick to perceive. Faced with the same brand of parental authority and resourcefulness that they meet in other areas of their home experience and given adequate substitutes in terms of comparable Jewish ceremonials, children would by no means make a special issue of this particular request. With many Jewish parents, the "Christmas problem" is in the same category as the "sex problem": the child makes a perfectly simple and normal request (for sex information—or for a Christmas tree) and the parents, who have their own emotional involvements in such matters, attribute unwarranted significance to the whole affair. We point to this, not by way of condensation, but rather in appraisal of a cold fact that the "Christmas tree problem" arises out of a negative condition in our parents rather than a positive devotion to our Jewish children, to the inherent esthetic qualities of a bedecked and betinseled fir tree.

II

Some parents rationalize their observance of Christmas by maintaining, usually with fervor, that Christmas is not a religious but rather a folk holiday. Many of our public schools justify their celebrations of Christmas on the same grounds. In this connection we must consider the incontrovertible fact that Christmas is one of the major events in every Christian church program in America. Even our public school celebrations (presumably "nonsectarian") include a "star of Bethlehem" on the tree and revolve about stories of the nativity, etc. Christmas carols are lovely melodies but their texts are neither general nor secular but specifically Christian.

Other parents admit the religious foundations of Christmas but justify its observance by Jews on the grounds of the widespread commercialization of the holiday. It takes on the aspect of a national holiday, they say. Merchants gear their business to it; cities decorate streets and buildings and hold community contests for home decoration, etc. We would agree that Jewish children need not be forced to shut their eyes to the beauty of Christmas decorations nor their ears to the charm of Christmas carols. Parents might well make a point of taking their children out to see the most beautifully adorned streets and residences of their Christian neighbors. This can be done exactly as children are exposed to many other things of beauty which, for one reason or another, they cannot possess. That Christmas is beautiful does not alter its essentially Christian character nor justify its adoption by self-respecting Jews.

III

In some Jewish homes the Christmas tree is introduced because, parents tell us, the child who wants one and is deprived of it is made to feel that he is *different.* "We want him to feel that he is an American just like his neighbors and playmates." We repeat the point made earlier in this discussion that this is a typical parental rationalization having little or nothing to do with the child's attitude. For, though children do indeed feel the need for belonging to the group and the urge to conform to its patterns, they learn very early that not all individuals or families or groups live by the same pattern. Let these apprehensive parents ask themselves: "Do we permit our child to do everything our neighbors' children do? Would we think of letting our child go to the movies every night just because Mary and Johnny do?" The basic fact is—and it is a principle that should be made clear to every child at an early age—that *families do things differently.* Meal times differ; spending money is handled in different ways; regulations vary from family to family as to toys, movies, vacations, bedtime, punishment, etc. There is obviously something peculiar which suddenly impels parents to fit into their neighbors' pattern when the month of December approaches.

Some children will continue to ask for Christmas trees as they continue to ask for candy before dinner. Reasonable parents and those who have not lost their sense of Jewish dignity will meet the request with calm and common sense. They will point out with dignity that, as Jews, we have our own religious and cultural tradition, that Christmas is therefore not our holiday though the trees and lights and colored decorations may delight our eyes as well. Such parents will not knuckle under at the first childish protest nor grasp at straws to save their children from the inevitable discovery that they are Jews. They will be aware that the "Christmas tree problem" is not a disease but only a periodic symptom of a much more general spiritual ailment.

IV

But what, now, of the child? Will Jewish children who are denied a Christmas tree fall prey to all these conflicts? Will they resent the Jewishness that deprives them of Christmas gaiety and Christmas presents? The answer must depend upon the kind of Jewish home in which the children live. If, in exchange for Christmas, the children's Jewishness gives them not one but eight days of *Chanukah,* with *Chanukah* gifts not once but on each of the eight nights [and if, in addition, it fills their lives with the rich and colorful ceremonials which children love: *Shabbat* with candles and *Kiddush* and *Havdalah* in the deepening dusk; the fun and beauty of the *sukah; Purim* with masks and greggers and presents; a *seder* with questions and singing and *afikoman;* and, throughout the year, enchanting tales of Jewish heroes and heroines and lilting Hebrew songs which children love to sing—if being Jewish offers these pleasures and satisfactions —adults call them compensations], then to miss out on Christmas will certainly leave no scar on the children's personalities and will create no conflict or complex about being "different" from the majority.

The parent, however, who denies a child a Christmas tree "on principle" and offers nothing in its stead may have genuine cause for concern. Children of such parents all too often are unhappy; they do have a sense of shame about their being different from, which to them means *inferior to,* their non-Jewish friends.

The question therefore is not whether or not to have a Christmas tree. This is but part of the larger problem of dramatizing Jewish values and making them meaningful in the lives of our children. It is not something that can be accomplished . . . when the Christmas spirit is already in the air. It is a matter for more sustained thinking and for all-year-round preparation. It involves rethinking our Jewish ceremonial tradition and, in most instances, reeducating Jewish parents. It means that parents must learn to capitalize on every occasion in the Jewish calendar for making Jewishness pleasant and attractive and desirable to their children. . . . Those of us who value our children's happiness will have to prepare our answer to the Christmas challenge in terms of intensified and beautified Jewish living through the twelve months of the year.

The Reconstructionist, December 28, 1951.

WHY NO CHRISTMAS TREE

A Letter from a Jewish Convert to Her Christian Mother

My Dear Mother:

Last summer before I took the final steps to be converted to Judaism, how earnestly we tried to reassure each other that the problems of different religions, which so often confound and dismay, surely could not build barriers between a mother and a daughter who love each other dearly. But at the same time we agreed that there would arise many questions which would seem difficult to solve. And now we come for the first time to the question of Christmas.

It seems that a quest for the real and deep meanings of life can sometimes involve people who love each other in very poignant situations; but perhaps a test of the loving is in the grace with which these situations can be met. To feel that I am hurting you hurts me more than you could know and that is why I want to write this letter to try to tell you how I feel about not having Christmas for the children.

I know you think I am being extreme and even stubborn about Christmas. The other day you said that Christmas does not even seem like a religious holiday and it occurred to me that as a Christian

I would have said the same thing—which is a very sad commentary upon the way that we have been Christians for a long time. Actually, Christmas is the most profoundly religious day in the whole Christian calendar, the moment for the deepest avowals of faith and belief.

I have found that as long as you are not sure what you believe, it doesn't seem to matter too much; but when you begin to know what you believe it begins to matter a great deal. And then to act at variance with that belief becomes a thing that is bound directly to your whole feeling of personal integrity. I don't think that this can seem so strange to you because, after all, you were the one who molded the way that I should feel about life. There was no teaching that ever received greater emphasis than that people should somehow attain the courage of their convictions; and you did not teach me to imagine that it would always be easy.

To be Jews all year except at Christmas time is the sort of a compromise of which I would not be proud; it is the sort of action that would symbolically nullify the meanings of both Judaism and Christianity. I know what you are thinking—that children understand nothing of meanings so how could it be serving any good purpose to deny them the happiness that Christmas brings?

It is of their happiness that I am thinking—not a momentary or a seasonal happiness but the kind that is built into a life. Because I want their happiness so much. I know better than ever before how much you always wanted happiness for me—how you worked for it, sacrificed for it, and planned for it. And it is one of those strange paradoxes of life that I should have found it in a way that you do not understand. But this much I want you to know, I have found a deep abiding happiness in my wholehearted acceptance of the Jewish faith, a happiness that comes from a real and irresistable sense of spiritual identity. And, because I feel these things so keenly, I think that I can make them richly and beautifully realized in the lives of my children. I know there is something in you that resists this feeling, something which keeps maintaining that it isn't easy to be a Jew. It isn't easy to be a Jew if you hate being one; and it isn't easy to respect a Jew who hates being a Jew. But a Jew to whom the meanings of faith are real has a heritage that is priceless, even above the price that must be paid for it.

You contend that Santa Claus and the Christmas tree are symbolically unrelated to the religious aspects of Christmas. Yet these are, undeniably, the symbols of Christmas; without Christmas they would not exist. Such is the inescapable thing about symbols; you must accept them in relation to what they represent, however obtusely, or not accept them at all.

I wish I could give you some opposite example to make you see how this works out. There is, for instance, one Jewish holiday called *Sukot,* at which time it is traditional for Jewish families to construct in their yards small booths which they leave open at the top so they may see the stars and which they adorn with the fruits of the harvest. The *Sukot* booth is to remind Jews that in just such rude shelters their ancestors lived in the wilderness as God brought them out of Egypt. And it is adorned with the fruits to show their thankfulness for God's care in providing for their needs.

A very beautiful custom, you may say. Yes, but can you imagine that a Christian father living next door to a Jewish family would try to construct such a booth in his own backyard, however urgently his own child might clamor for such a playhouse? He might, the next week, buy $100 worth of lumber to build a playhouse, but he would not try to build the sort of a booth that the Jews had made. He would understand that, in some way which might not be comprehensible to him, it was bound with their religion.

In this case where we are not so sentimentally involved, it is easy to see that to separate a symbol from what it symbolizes merely to enjoy it would be, somehow, a spiritually dishonest thing.

I wish you would not have the feeling that by not having Christmas I am depriving the children of so much. No one knows better than I do how children love holidays, how they love specialness and festivity. But surely you have discovered how many holidays are woven into the Jewish year, each with its own customs and meanings and own "specialness." Why even Friday night is special with the lighting of candles, the breaking of bread, the drinking of wine, and the saying of the blessings to usher in the Sabbath.

The holiday that most nearly coincides in time with Christmas is *Chanukah,* the Feast of Lights. It lasts eight days and commemorates the first time in history that men took up arms to fight for religious freedom. The legend goes that, when Judah the Maccabee came triumphant to the Temple at Jerusalem, his first purpose was to rekindle the Eternal Light which is never extinguished in a Jewish house of worship. He found only the cruse of oil that had not been desecrated by the pagans, and it contained only enough oil to burn for one day. But miraculously it burned for eight days, and so the Feast of Lights is observed for eight days. Its special symbol is an eight-pronged candelabrum [called a *chanukiah*] in which one candle is lighted the first night and one more each succeeding night until, on the last night, all eight are burning. And the whole eight days are occasions for festive observance and gift-giving.

Please do not imagine that I intend to ban Christmas from the lives of the children as if it did not exist. After all, Christmas is in the very air we breathe for over a month. They have it at school, over the radio, downtown, everywhere. They will inevitably participate in the mood of Christmas and enjoy the mood that it engenders among people; and perhaps they will begin to learn that it is possible in life to appreciate many things that are not claimed as one's very own. But what is most personal and basic and fundamental in their own home, what is most essentially the expression of their own spirit will be the Feast of Lights. The acts of faith will be Jewish acts of faith because they are Jews.

And so, my dear mother, there it is. This has been my very earnest effort to make you understand my feelings. Please think very hard about what I have said and see if you still feel that I am wrong. I so sincerely hope not. I do hope that the season of Christmas and *Chanukah* can be a truly joyous one for all of us in which we can share without restraint the beauties that are implicit in both of these religious holidays, each of which was conceived as a part of the human avowal of God.

Your loving daughter,
Deborah

The Reconstructionist, December 28, 1951.

CHRISTMAS AND THE JEWISH CHILD

by Dr. Alice Ginott

Christmas may be fun for children, but it can be a mixed blessing for parents. Children's demands seem to grow beyond reason during the holiday season—and so do parents' irritation and guilt. As one mother puts it: "I can't take my son to any store. Whatever he sees, he wants. He likes anything that starts with the letter 'a'—a bicycle, a gun, a transistor radio, a fishing rod." One father confides: "I feel bad when I have to say 'no' to my little girl. She looks at me with her sad eyes and cries. Her tears accuse me: 'You're a bad Daddy.' I usually give in to her, then feel annoyed with myself. My choice seems to be feeling guilty or angry."

For Jewish parents, the "Christmas problem" is even more complicated. Not only would their children like to be in charge of the family budget during the holidays, but they also want to be the arbiters of the family's beliefs. They beg, cajole, and plead that they be allowed to celebrate Christmas with everyone else, even though it is not their holiday.

Many Jewish parents find it hard to refuse. They borrow the style if not the substance of Christmas and, believing that they can take the Christian religion out of Christmas, create an artificial holiday for their children.

It is important that parents not treat a wish as a need. Children have a right to expect their parents to take care of their needs. We have great latitude about wishes. Some we may want to satisfy, others we only need to acknowledge. A wish is neither a command nor a demand. It is a request that we accept but not necessarily gratify.

Jewish children have no need to celebrate Christmas. They may wish to be part of the excitement—to dream of a white Christmas with all the other children. The child may want the pleasure of decorating a Christmas tree and to wake up on Christmas morning pretending that those gifts were left by Santa Claus. But neither the child's physical nor emotional well-being depends on having these desires gratified.

On the contrary, when Jewish parents emphasize Christmas at the expense of *Chanukah,* they deprive their children of an opportunity to feel proud of their past and to develop a positive attitude towards their roots.

Chanukah stands as a symbol of the Jewish people's struggle to maintain their spiritual identity against superior forces; it was the first battle for religious freedom.

When, less than 200 years before the birth of Christ, Antiochus, the Greek conqueror, forbade the Jews to practice their faith, a small group of men—led by Judah the Maccabee—rose up in arms and, after three years of fighting, entered Jerusalem and purified the Temple. *Chanukah,* the Feast of Lights, commemorates this event and celebrates the miracle of the Temple lights, which burned for eight days even though there was only enough oil for one.

And so for eight days Jews celebrate. Each evening they light one additional candle in a candelabrum called a menorah or *chanukiah,* offering a prayer of thanks for their spiritual survival. It is a happy holiday and it is a children's holiday. There is singing, gift-giving, and playing of games, such as the one with a spinning top, or *dreidel,* which gives children the opportunity to win money called *Chanukah gelt.*

Many Jewish families give a big *Chanukah* party to which they invite Christian friends and their children. One woman told me how surprised she was to be told by a young man who had been to her *Chanukah* party twenty years before—when he was a little boy— how envious he was of the warmth in her home. He wished he had been born a Jew so that he could celebrate *Chanukah.*

Yet for many Jewish children, their holiday pales by comparison. They cannot help but be swept up by the excitement of Christmas. For over a month, Christmas carols fill the air. Store windows are transformed into a Christmas wonderland. Everyone seems to be involved in the warmth and glow. It is easy for a Jewish child to get the impression that, during Christmas, Christians have more fun than anybody.

Naturally, children want to be part of the fun. They don't like being different. They don't like being deprived. They don't like being left out. And they don't like being cheated. As one eight-year-old told me: "It's hard to be Jewish during Christmas. It's not too bad when *Chanukah* comes at the same time, but this year it will be very lonely." And a ten-year-old girl, when asked how she felt about Christmas, said: "It feels like all the people are Christians. I know I shouldn't feel that way, but I can't help it. Sometimes I wish I could be Christian, too."

What is a Jewish parent to do?

Understand and sympathize with the children's predicament by acknowledging their feelings: "It's not easy to be Jewish during Christmas. Everyone seems to be celebrating Christmas except you. But it's nice to see people being more friendly and helpful, to enjoy the beautiful store windows, and to get into the holiday spirit." Or: "I know you wish you could have a Christmas tree like your friends. You'd know exactly how to decorate it. And how much fun it would be to get up Christmas morning and find all the presents you ever wanted under the Christmas tree. But Christmas is a Christian holi- day. We are Jews. We celebrate *Chanukah.*"

Children who feel understood feel loved. It helps them to tolerate frustration and stops them from feeling sorry for themselves for not being able to celebrate Christmas. Children do not need to be given everything they want; they need to be given permission to want. When parents verbalize the wishes of their children, they give them that permission.

Parents who feel comfortable being Jewish do not need to compensate or compete, nor do they imitate. They are not defensive nor do they feel guilty. They can accept the fact that being Jewish in a predominantly Christian country may have its temptations—and help their children cope with them. As one boy so aptly put it when asked how he felt being Jewish during Christmas: "I'm the luckiest boy. I love all the presents I get for *Chanukah* and I don't have to go to school on Christmas."

Ladies' Home Journal, December 1977.

POTATO LATKE RECIPE

by Mildred Kessler

1 large onion	salt and pepper to taste
7 medium potatoes	½ cup *matzah* meal
2 eggs	vegetable oil

Grate potatoes either by hand or in a food processor. Grate onion. Drain liquid. Mix all the ingredients together except the vegetable oil. Heat the vegetable oil in large frying pan. Drop about 1 tablespoon of mixture for each *latke* into a hot frying pan and fry over medium heat until crisp and golden on each side.

This can be served with applesauce, sour cream, or both.

For further information on *Chanukah,* see *The Jewish Home,* Book 3.

CONVERSION

Resource Sheet 17

GLOSSARY

Ger/Gioret—

Gerut—

Halachah—

Kabbalat Ol Mitzvot—

Tevilah—

Milah—

LETTER TO OBADIAH THE PROSELYTE

Thus says Moses, the son of Rabbi Maimon, one of the exiles from Jerusalem, who lived in Spain:

I received the question of the master Obadiah, the wise and learned proselyte, may the Lord reward him for his work, may a perfect recompense be bestowed upon him by the Lord of Israel, under whose wings he has sought cover.

You ask me if you, too, are allowed to say in the blessings and prayers you offer alone or in the congregation: *"Our* God" and "God of *our* fathers," "You who have sanctified *us* through Your commandments," "You who have separated *us,* " "You who have chosen *us,* " "You who have inherited *us,* " "You who have brought *us* out of the land of Egypt," "You who have worked miracles to *our* fathers," and more of this kind.

Yes, you may say all this in the prescribed order and not change it in the least. In the same way as every Jew by birth says his blessing and prayer, you, too, shall bless and pray alike, whether you are alone or pray in the congregation. The reason for this is that Abraham our Father taught the people, opened their minds, and revealed to them the true faith and the unity of God; he rejected the idols and abolished their adoration; he brought many children under the wings of the Divine Presence; he gave them counsel and advice and ordered his sons and the members of his household after him to keep the ways of the Lord forever, as it is written, "For I have known him to the end that he may command his children and his household after him, that they may keep the way of the Lord, to do righteousness and justice." (Genesis 18:19) Ever since then whoever adopts Judaism and confesses the unity of the Divine Name, as it is prescribed in the Torah, is counted among the disciples of Abraham our Father, peace be with him. These men are Abraham's household, and he it is who converted them to righteousness.

In the same way as he converted his contemporaries through his words and teaching, he converts future generations through the testament he left to his children and household after him. Thus Abraham our Father, peace be with him, is the father of his pious posterity who keep his ways, and the father of his disciples and of all proselytes who adopt Judaism.

Therefore you shall pray, "Our God" and "God of our fathers," because Abraham, peace be with him, is *your* father. And you shall pray, "You who have taken for his own our fathers," for the land has been given to Abraham, as it is said, "Arise, walk through the land in the length of it and in the breadth of it; for I will give it to you." (Genesis 13:17) As to the words, "You who have brought us out of the land of Egypt" or "You who have done miracles to our fathers" these you may change, if you will, and say, "You who have brought Israel out of the land of Egypt" and "You who have done miracles to Israel." If, however, you do not change them, it is no transgression because, since you have come under the wings of the Divine Presence and confessed the Lord, no difference exists between you and us, and all miracles done to us have been done as it were to us and to you. Thus it is said in the Book of Isaiah, "Neither let the son of the stranger, that has joined himself to the Lord, speak, saying, 'The Lord has utterly separated me from His people'." (56:3) There is no difference whatever between you and us. You shall certainly say the blessing, "Who has chosen us," "Who has given us," "Who has taken us for Your own," and "Who has separated us"; for the Creator, may He be extolled, has indeed chosen you and separated you from the nations and given you the Torah. For the Torah has been given to us and to the proselytes, as it is said, "One ordinance shall be both for you of the congregation and also for the stranger that sojourns with you, an ordinance for ever in your generations; as you are, so shall the stranger be before the Lord." (Numbers 15:15) Know that our fathers, when they came out of Egypt, were mostly idolaters, they had mingled with the pagans in Egypt and imitated their way of life, until the Holy One, may He be blessed, sent Moses our Teacher, the master of all prophets, who separated us from the nations and brought us under the wings of the Divine Presence, us and all proselytes, and gave to all of us one Law.

Do not consider your origin as inferior. While we are the descendants of Abraham, Isaac, and Jacob, you derive from Him through whose word the world was created. As is said by Isaiah, "One shall say, I am the Lord's, and another shall call himself by the name of Jacob." (Isaiah 44:5)

Twersky, Isadore, ed. *A Maimonides Reader.* New York: Behrman House, Inc., 1972.

Resource Sheet 19

CONVERSION SERVICE

Two persons, representative of the congregation, should be witnesses of the ceremony. It is suggested that the service be conducted in the synagogue, preferably before the open ark.

בָּרוּךְ הַבָּא בְּשֵׁם יְיָ בֵּרַכְנוּכֶם מִבֵּית יְיָ.

Baruch haba beshem Adonai berachenuchem mibet Adonai.
Blessed be you who come in the name of the Lord: We bless you from the House of the Lord.

Our God and Father, with grateful hearts we thank You for many blessings. We thank You that You do reveal Your truth to humanity. Above all, we praise You for the gift of the Torah, which has ever been a lamp unto our feet and a light unto our path. We recall with reverence and gratitude all those of the seed of Abraham who have been faithful unto You and those who of their own choice have sought to serve You in the faith and fellowship of Israel.

Be near us in this solemn hour. Grant, O God, Your loving favor to . . . , as in this holy place we welcome him/her into Jewish life. Help him/her to live in fidelity to the decision he/she has made, and to the promise he/she is about to utter. May he/she always find joy in the fulfillment of Your Torah and enduring satisfaction in the practice of Judaism. Vouchsafe unto him/her many years of strength and happiness as a worthy son/daughter of the synagogue. Blessed are You, O Lord, in whose presence is fullness of joy. Amen.

The rabbi delivers a brief charge to the convert and then asks the following questions, to which the convert responds:
1. Do you of your own free will seek admittance into the Jewish faith?
2. Have you given up your former faith and severed all other religious affiliation?

3. Do you pledge your loyalty to Judaism and to the Jewish people amid all circumstances and conditions?

4. Do you promise to establish a Jewish home and to participate actively in the life of the synagogue and of the Jewish community?

5. If you should be blessed with children, do you promise to rear them in the Jewish faith?

When the convert has answered "yes" to each of the questions, the rabbi says: I summon you then to pronounce the affirmation by which the Jew lives and which is on his lips even in his last moment on earth.

The convert recites the *Shema:*

שְׁמַע יִשְׂרָאֵל: יְיָ אֱלֹהֵינוּ, יְיָ אֶחָד.

Shema Yisrael Adonai Elohenu Adonai Echad.
Hear O Israel: the Lord our God, the Lord is One.

בָּרוּךְ שֵׁם כְּבוֹד מַלְכוּתוֹ לְעוֹלָם וָעֶד

Baruch shem kevod malchuto le'olam va'ed.
Praised be His name whose glorious kingdom is for ever and ever.

The following readings may be included:
   You shall love the Lord, your God, with all your heart, with all your soul, and with all your might. And these words, which I command you this day, shall be upon your heart. You shall teach them diligently unto your children and shall speak of them when you sit in your house, when you walk by the way, when you lie down and when you rise up. You shall bind them for a sign upon your hand, and they shall be for frontlets between your eyes. You shall write them upon the doorposts of your house and upon your gates: That you may remember and do all My commandments and be holy unto your God.

If the convert is a woman:
   And Ruth said: Entreat me not to leave you, and to return from following after you; for where you go, I will go; and where you lodge, I will lodge; your people shall be my people, and your God my God; where you die, will I die, and there will I be buried; the Lord do so to me, and more also, if aught but death part you and me. (Ruth 1:16–17)

All present standing:

Let us adore the ever-living God and render praise unto Him who spread out the heavens and established the earth, whose glory is revealed in the heavens above and whose greatness is manifest throughout the world. He is our God: there is none else.

וַאֲנַחְנוּ כּוֹרְעִים וּמִשְׁתַּחֲוִים וּמוֹדִים לִפְנֵי מֶלֶךְ מַלְכֵי הַמְּלָכִים הַקָּדוֹשׁ בָּרוּךְ הוּא.

Va'anachnu korim umishtachavim umodim lifnei Melech malechei hamelachim Hakadosh baruch Hu.

We bow the head in reverence, and worship the King of kings, the Holy One, praised be He.

May the time not be distant, O God, when Your name shall be worshiped in all the earth, when unbelief shall disappear and error be no more. We fervently pray that the day may come when all men shall invoke Your name, when corruption and evil shall give way to purity and goodness, when superstition shall no longer enslave the mind, nor idolatry blind the eye, when all inhabitants of the earth shall know that to You alone every knee must bend and every tongue give homage. O may all, created in Your image, recognize that they are brethren, so that, one in spirit and one in fellowship, they may be forever united before You. Then shall Your kingdom be established on earth and the word of Your ancient seer be fulfilled: The Lord will reign for ever and ever.

On that day the Lord shall be One and His name shall be One.

The rabbi takes the convert's hand, saying:

May God strengthen you in the solemn commitment you have made. As a rabbi in Israel, and with the consent of these witnesses, I welcome you warmly and joyously into our faith and fellowship; and I confer upon you the Hebrew name. . . .

The rabbi places his hand on the head of the convert and says:

יְבָרֶכְךָ יְיָ וְיִשְׁמְרֶךָ,
יָאֵר יְיָ פָּנָיו אֵלֶיךָ וִיחֻנֶּךָּ,
יִשָּׂא יְיָ פָּנָיו אֵלֶיךָ וְיָשֵׂם לְךָ שָׁלוֹם.

Yevarechecha Adonai veyishmerecha
Ya'er Adonai panav elecha vichuneka

Yisa Adonai panav elecha veyasem lecha shalom.
May the Lord bless you and keep you
May the Lord cause His countenance to shine upon you and be
 gracious unto you
May the Lord lift up His countenance unto you and give you peace.
 Amen.

Or

יְשַׁלֵּם יְיָ פָּעֳלֵךְ. וּתְהִי מַשְׂכֻּרְתֵּךְ שְׁלֵמָה מֵעִם יְיָ אֱלֹהֵי
יִשְׂרָאֵל. אֲשֶׁר־בָּאת לַחֲסוֹת תַּחַת כְּנָפָיו.

Yeshalem Adonai po'olech utehi maskuretech shelemah me'im Adonai Elohei Yisrael. Asher bat lachasot tachat kenafav.
The Lord recompense your work, and be your reward complete from
the Lord, the God of Israel, under whose wings you come to take
refuge.

After the ceremony, a certificate of conversion, properly signed by
the rabbi and countersigned by the witnesses and by the convert,
should be read before it is handed to the convert. A duplicate of the
certificate, properly signed and countersigned, should be put into the
archives of the congregation represented by the officiating rabbi.

Rabbi's Manual. New York: Central Conference of American Rabbis, 1961.

Resource Sheet 20

THE CONVERSION OF CAITLIN O'SULLIVAN

by Daniel Syme

On January 10, 1981 Caitlin O'Sullivan became a Jew. Her conversion ceremony took place during a *Shabbat* morning service at New York City's Stephen Wise Free Synagogue, perhaps the first public conversion ceremony ever in Manhattan. I was there—as her rabbi and as her friend.

March, 1980
My first meeting with Caitlin O'Sullivan was an accident. The then embryonic Task Force on Reform Jewish Outreach of the Union of American Hebrew Congregations and the Central Conference of American Rabbis had decided to sponsor a weekend program at the UAHC's House of Living Judaism in New York. Registration for the program, originally intended solely for recent converts to Judaism, was lagging somewhat behind expectations. Accordingly, I was asked to recruit participants from Introduction to Judaism classes in the UAHC's New York conversion course program. Doubting the potential efficacy of my efforts, I nonetheless spoke to one class and distributed flyers for the *shabbaton.*

No more than ten minutes after completing my "pitch," I had one application in hand. Caitlin O'Sullivan had made a decision to examine Judaism a little more closely. I remember how struck I was at the time with her confidence, her enthusiasm, her candor. This is, I thought, a remarkable woman.

April, 1980
During the Outreach weekend, Caitlin O'Sullivan spoke very little. She participated knowledgeably in *Shabbat* services and even offered a spontaneous closing prayer. But mostly she listened intently to the statements of others, absorbing, concentrating. Finally, on Saturday night, Caitlin shared her personal story.

She had been raised as a Catholic in a community on the West

Coast. After a deeply disillusioning family trauma during her high school years, Caitlin and others in her family fell away from the church. Caitlin, especially, began to examine other religions—particularly Judaism. Now, as an adult, after studying on her own for many years, she had taken a second step in the direction of Judaism by enrolling in the UAHC's conversion course. She made it clear that her mind was not yet made up, that she was still thinking and learning and doing Jewishly. In effect, she was "trying Judaism on," seeing how it felt. There was no sense of urgency to her search. After all, conversion was more than a casual decision. It represented a major life commitment.

She concluded her remarks. No one in the room moved. No one coughed. No one yawned or stretched. We all knew that, in a very real sense, we were witnessing the formation of a potentially new Jewish soul. We were deeply moved and touched by this young woman, who knew herself so well and who was so determined to maintain her intellectual and religious integrity. We wished her well on her search, quietly hoping that Judaism would one day be blessed by her addition to our people and to our faith.

April–December, 1980
The weekend came to a close. Caitlin left us, but I continued to receive reports of her "progress." She called from time to time, just to say hello. Mutual friends told me of her constant presence at Stephen Wise Free Synagogue. Then, just after the High Holy Days, Caitlin appeared in my office. She had decided to embrace Judaism and to visit the *mikveh* as a prelude to the service. Most significantly, however, Caitlin O'Sullivan had seized upon an idea she had first heard expressed at the New York Outreach weekend. She wanted a public conversion, and she asked me to participate and to offer a blessing on her behalf.

The notion of conversion to Judaism in the presence of the entire congregation has been shared and popularized primarily by Lydia Kukoff, an adult education specialist, teacher, and Outreach program consultant to many Jewish organizations.

Her logic is inescapable. Born Jews have never been made privy to the process of conversion. Indeed, conversion has been something "we don't talk about," consigned to the rabbi's study or a deserted chapel. That, Lydia Kukoff asserts, is a mistake. The community needs to be part of conversion, to see thinking, caring men and women, who are *choosing* Judaism. No ambivalence, no embarrassment, no hang-ups. Judaism is their first choice. What a boon to Jewish pride! What a spur to adult Jewish learning! What a weapon against stereotypes and ethnic prejudice!

And, what a support to the new Jew! A community bearing witness to this powerful moment, with no preconditions and no judgments. Lydia Kukoff has crisscrossed North America, bringing her message to dozens of communities, large and small. She planted the seed—and Caitlin O'Sullivan, hearing her at the Outreach weekend, decided to bring it to fruition.

I told Caitlin that I'd be honored to be part of her conversion and suggested that we talk further about how best to structure the service and about setting a date. To my amazement, I then learned that Caitlin planned on putting the entire service together; assigning parts to the rabbis, conducting a major portion of the service herself, selecting the music, delivering the sermon—everything was to be carefully planned and sensitively done. She had a date when no *Bar* or *Bat Mitzvah* was scheduled. That *Shabbat* would be hers alone.

December, 1980
In mid-December, the Task Force on Reform Jewish Outreach sponsored a second New York weekend. Caitlin attended along with four other "alumni" of the April *shabbaton.* In contrast to her quiet, almost reserved manner eight months earlier, Caitlin had now become a confident, articulate "Jew in process." Though her formal conversion was still a month away, there was no doubt that many weekend participants looked to Caitlin as a model, a resource, a friend. She issued a blanket invitation to the group to attend her conversion ceremony, and a number said they'd be there.

January 1, 1981
New Year's Day. Between football games, I suddenly realized that Caitlin's service was a week away—and I had not the slightest idea of what I intended to say to her in front of all those people. My rabbi's manual was no help. This had to be thoroughly personal.

Eight hours later I had a first draft. Over the next several days I shared it with at least a dozen colleagues and friends. Each made suggestions, changes, and additions. At last, by Thursday, I felt I knew how I wanted to say what I felt so deeply.

That night, Caitlin and I spoke by phone. She outlined the service. We talked through her personal declaration and the blessing itself. Then Caitlin dropped the bombshell. She was having second thoughts. She wasn't sure she was doing the right thing, and she was scared. Her parents were coming along with dozens of other friends and acquaintances whom she had invited, and the pressure was a little frightening. I did my best to reassure her that her feelings were normal and natural. This was, after all, a life-altering step, every bit as significant as a marriage. And, I said with a lump in my throat, the absolute worst that could happen would be to delay the ceremony. After thirty minutes on the phone, we agreed that Caitlin should call a friend who had chosen Judaism, just to talk. The call was made. By Friday, to my relief, Caitlin once again felt solid about her decision.

Friday night, January 9, 1981
I didn't sleep more than three hours. I kept going over my remarks, pacing the floor, making sure that I had done as much as I could to make the next morning's service as meaningful and moving as possible. I finally drifted off at about 3:00 A.M. but was up again at six. I kept thinking about how much insight the Torah has. Wherever in the Torah it says "And he got up early in the morning," it indicates that the person is facing an important and somewhat frightening task —Abraham preparing to take Isaac to Mount Moriah, for example, or Jacob preparing to meet his brother Esau after many years.

I finally gave up on sleep and left for the synagogue at 8:00 A.M.

January 10, 1981
When services don't begin until 10:30 A.M., you may be interested to know that most temples are locked at 8:15 in the morning. The Stephen Wise Free Synagogue is no exception. There I was, dressed, ready for services, standing outside in the cold, and feeling very silly. Finally, a security guard let me in, and I sat inside for almost two hours. About ten o'clock, Caitlin arrived. Together with everyone participating in the service, we went over the order one last time. Before I knew it, it was time to begin.

My throat felt dry. I hadn't been this nervous since officiating at my first *Berit Milah.* It took place in a hospital operating room, and the *mohel* and I both wore hospital gowns and surgical masks. I was a rabbinic student at the time and had my rabbi's manual clutched in my hand as we began. Disaster! Every time I breathed, my glasses fogged up, obscuring my sight of the various *berachot.* I kept wiping them off, becoming so hysterical in the process that after chanting the *Kiddush* I forgot I had a mask on—and poured the entire cup of wine down the front of my hospital gown!

I thought of that moment as I, Caitlin, and others participating in the services walked up onto the *bimah*. I was terrified! Looking out at the congregation, I was surprised and pleased. There were members of the congregation, faculty members, and students of the Hebrew Union College-Jewish Institute of Religion in New York, numerous alumni of the New York Outreach weekends, men and women who had been part of Caitlin's conversion class, people from my apartment building in New York who had been intrigued by my description of what was to happen, and, of course, Caitlin's family, seated in the very first row, eyes riveted to her every move, giving silent support and encouragement. The sanctuary was full.

Rabbis Edward Klein and Balfour Brickner of the Stephen Wise Free Synagogue conducted the first part of the service, explaining the history and significance of certain *berachot* for the benefit of all in attendance. Caitlin read a number of sections as well. Then came the Torah service. Caitlin chanted the blessings after which Rabbi Brickner read and commented on the *sidrah*. Caitlin read a special *haftarah* from the Book of Ruth, with the *berachot* before and after chanted by her conversion course instructor, Rabbi A. Bruce Goldman.

At last the magical moment had arrived. The congregation waited expectantly. There was not a sound in the entire sanctuary. Caitlin and I stood at the *bimah*. My hands were shaking, and I decided to share my feelings with Caitlin.

"Caitlin," I said, "I want you to know that I'm scared to death. I've never done this before."

"That's all right," she replied. "Neither have I." The congregation roared. The tension broken, I continued:

"Caitlin, in the presence of your family and friends, before this open ark, and witnessed by this entire congregation, your journey begins.

"Every Jewish experience until this moment has been only a prelude to the challenge you are about to accept. All the searching, all the study, all the doubts and fears, the joy and exhilaration of discovery and decision culminate in this instant of re-creation.

"You are about to become a Jewish newborn, entitled thereby to an extra measure of love and caring from the Jewish community. We are obligated to nurture and to nourish you.

"But you, in turn, take on new and awesome responsibilities. You have committed yourself and your future to Jewish living and to the creation of a personal Jewish past. You will continue to study and do, learn and experience, growing each day as a unique and special person. We are also now dependent upon you for our physical and spiritual Jewish survival. You will influence generations of Jewish children and adults. You will teach them by your example and invest them with Jewish identity. From this moment on, then, Caitlin, our destiny is inextricably bound up with yours.

"As a rabbi, as one who cares deeply about Judaism, the Jewish people, and the Jewish future, but above all as a friend, who has come to admire and respect you, it is now my privilege to recognize your formal entry into Judaism."

At this point, Caitlin's friend, David Kleiman stepped forward and placed a *talit* around Caitlin's shoulders, his personal gift to her on this occasion. The three of us then walked to the open ark. Caitlin took the Torah in her arms and cradled it as I spoke.

"In the presence of this congregation I ask you to hold this Torah and to recite the *Shema*, the watch-word of our faith."

Caitlin recited the *Shema* in a strong, clear voice, then sang it with her eyes closed, wrapped in her *talit*. A chill ran up my spine.

I spoke to her again: "In the presence of this community I ask if you freely cast your lot with that of the Jewish people from this day forth."

She replied: "I do."

I responded: "In accordance with Jewish custom, I give unto you the Hebrew name you have chosen as your own: *Elisheva*—God Is My Oath—*Elisheva bat Avraham vesarah.* May it become a name honored in the household of Israel."

I then asked Caitlin to stand at the *bimah* and to declare her acceptance of Judaism. The congregation leaned forward, eager to hear this woman who had already moved and touched them so. Caitlin began:

"I, Caitlin O'Sullivan, at this moment embrace Judaism into my being. I do this freely, openly, and with great joy before the assembled congregation as a pledge to God and humanity. I cast off the necessity of intercession and undertake the responsibility of a direct, active, and immediate relationship to the Power of the universe.

"I honor and thank my parents and my heritage for giving me life and the strength to commit myself to a belief that is my fulfillment, but different from theirs.

"I approach the Jewish people with deep love and ask their acceptance of me as a member of the Jewish community.

"I commit the totality of my strength and loyalty to support and defend the Jewish people amid all circumstances to the absolute limit of my being.

"I pledge to live each day within a Jewish framework:

"To create and maintain a Jewish home.

"To observe the traditions and customs of Judaism within my home and in public worship to the extent that these practices further and enhance my love of God and the Jewish people.

"To spend time in study and the pursuit of Jewish learning, developing the deepest possible understanding of Jewish law, language, thought, and culture in order to contribute to my spiritual development and to the future of Judaism.

"To love and serve other people, always striving to understand the meaning of commitment to another human being.

"To develop my individual gifts and talents to their highest potential as a fulfillment of the promise of creation.

"To allow beauty, harmony, and peace into my awareness alongside the struggle for achievement, remembering that joy and celebration are as exalted and beloved of God as study, work, and prayer."

Caitlin looked at me. She was finished. I looked out at the congregation. Many were in tears. I led Caitlin back to the ark, then spoke both to her and to all those in attendance.

"We who bear witness to this moment have, like you, been eternally transformed. We will never be the same again. We have been blessed through our participation in this, your moment. I therefore ask the entire congregation to join with you and with me in affirming the uniqueness of this day by reciting the *Shehecheyanu.*"

The congregation stood as one and recited the *Shehecheyanu.* It may have been my imagination, but I can't remember ever hearing it said quite so enthusiastically. A new Jewish soul had come into the world, and its spiritual parents rejoiced. Caitlin bowed her head, I offered the blessing, and then we gave one another a big hug. It was a moment that changed at least two lives.

Later in the service, Caitlin delivered the sermon. She spoke of the sort of experience to which every Jew might aspire.

"One Friday evening I decided I wanted to light *Shabbat* candles. I asked my friend if it was all right—was there anything wrong with it if I wasn't Jewish? He assured me that lightning would not strike me nor an earthquake swallow me up. He helped me learn the blessing and we talked about the various customs involved in the physical act of kindling the lights. I picked something that seemed to work with my personality and I did it. As I opened my eyes and beheld the light I had created, I was moved as I had never been moved in my life. In that moment I understood the concept of mystery, of spirit, of invoking a power greater than myself, through myself. I understood that by activating something very deep and personal, I could also touch something as incomprehensible as the light of the stars in the universe. In that moment I was changed forever, changed utterly."

She concluded: "My discovery of Judaism as a Jew has just begun. Judaism is multi-ethnic, multi-cultural, multi-national. The only limits to an expression of Jewish identity must necessarily be self-imposed. My explorations may take me far, far afield, I know not where. I have reached, I have struggled for knowledge and understanding, and now I am ready to begin."

No matter where life takes me as a rabbi, I do not believe I will ever again feel as I did on that *Shabbat* morning. The moment and the community met in a perfect union, electric, powerful, Jewish.

We are indeed fortunate. Caitlin O'Sullivan is a Jew. God grant that many others like her will opt for public conversion and thereby help born Jews see their faith and their people through new and fresh eyes.

Moment Magazine, Volume 6, Number 6, June 1981.

DEATH

Resource Sheet 21

GLOSSARY

Sheol—

Gan Eden—

Gehinom—

Kevod Hamet—

Taharah—

Tachrichim—

Chevrah Kadisha—

El Malei Rachamim—

Keriah—

Shivah—

Sheloshim—

Unveiling—

Yahrzeit—

Kaddish—

Yizkor—

Seudat Havra'ah—

Mitzvah—

Minyan—

Tsedakah—

Resource Sheet 22

TO HOLD WITH OPEN ARMS

by Milton Steinberg

It is a sound convention which requires that a sermon begin with a text—some verse from Scripture or from Rabbinic Literature—which summarizes the theme. But it is well to understand that a text is, after all, only the soul-experience of some man boiled down to the size of an epigram. At some time in the past a prophet or a saint met God, wrestled with good or evil, tasted of life and found it bitter or sweet, contemplated death, and then distilled the adventure into a single line for those that would come after him. That is a text.

But it is not only the great, the saints, the prophets, and the heroes who contemplate God, life, and death. We, too, the plainer folk of the world, live, love, laugh, and suffer, and by no means always on the surface. We, too, catch glimpses of eternity and the things that people do. Not only of Moses, but of us, too, it may be said, as Lowell put it: "Daily with souls that cringe and plot/We Sinais climb and know it not."

There are texts in us, too, in our commonplace experiences, if only we are wise enough to discern them.

One such experience, a textual experience, so to speak, fell to my lot not so long ago. There was nothing dramatic about its setting nor unusual in its circumstances. And yet to me it was a moment of discovery, almost of revelation.

Let me recount it very briefly, as befits a text. After a long illness, I was permitted for the first time to step out-of-doors. And as I crossed the threshold sunlight greeted me. This is my experience—all there is to it. And yet, so long as I live, I shall never forget that moment. It was mid-January—a time of cold and storm up north, but, in Texas, where I happened to be, a season much like our spring. The sky overhead was very blue, very clear, and very, very high. Not, I thought, the *shamayim*, heaven, but *shemei shamayim*, a heaven of heavens. A faint wind blew from off the western plains, cool and yet somehow tinged with warmth—like a dry, chilled wine. And, everywhere in the firmament above me, in the great vault between the earth and sky, on the pavements, the buildings—the golden glow of the sunlight. It touched me, too, with friendship, with warmth, with blessing. And as I basked in its glory there ran through my mind those wonderful words of the prophet about the sun which someday shall rise with healing on its wings.

In that instant I looked about me to see whether anyone else showed on his face the joy, almost the beatitude, I felt. But no, there they walked—men and women and children in the glory of the golden flood, and, so far as I could detect, there was none to give it heed. And then I remembered how often I, too, had been indifferent to sunlight, how often, preoccupied with petty and sometimes mean concerns, I had disregarded it. And I said to myself: "How precious is the sunlight but, alas, how careless of it are men." How precious —how careless. This has been a refrain sounding in me ever since.

It rang in my spirit when I entered my own home again after months of absence; when I heard from a nearby room the excited voices of my children at play; when I looked once more on the clear faces of some of my friends; when I was able for the first time to speak again from my pulpit in the name of our faith and tradition, to join in worship of the God who gives us so much of which we are so careless.

And a resolution crystallized within me. I said to myself that at the very first opportunity I would speak of this. I knew full well that it is a commonplace truth, that there is nothing clever about my private rediscovery of it, nothing ingenious about my way of putting it. But I was not interested in being original or clever or ingenious. I wanted only to remind my listeners, as I was reminded, to spend life wisely, not to squander it.

I wanted to say to the husbands and wives who love one another: "How precious is your lot in that it is one of love. Do not be, even for a moment, casual with your good fortune. Love one another while yet you may."

And to parents: "How precious is the gift of your children. Never, never be too busy for the wonder and miracle of them. They will be grown up soon enough and grown away, too."

We human beings, we frail reeds who are yet, as Pascal said, *thinking* reeds, *feeling* reeds, how precious are our endowments— minds to know, eyes to see, ears to listen, hearts to stir with pity, and to dream of justice and of a perfected world. How often are we indifferent to all these.

And we who are Jews and American, heirs of two great traditions, how fortunate our lot in both, and how blind we are to our double good fortune.

This is what struggled in me for utterance—as it struggled in Edna St. Vincent Millay when she cried out: "O world I cannot hold thee close enough."

I want to urge myself and all others to hold the world tight—to embrace life with all our hearts and all our souls and all our might. For it is precious, ineffably precious, and we are careless, wantonly careless of it.

And yet, when I first resolved to express all this, I knew that it was only a half-truth.

Could I have retained the sunlight no matter how hard I tried? Could I have prevented the sun from setting? Could I have kept even my own eyes from becoming satiated and bored with the glory of the day? That moment had to slip away. And, had I tried to hold on to it, what would I have achieved? It would have gone from me in any case. And I would have been left disconsolate, embittered, convinced that I had been cheated.

But it is not only the sunlight that must slip away—our youth goes also, our years, our children, our senses, our lives. This is the nature of things, an inevitability. And the sooner we make our peace with it the better. Did I urge myself a moment ago to hold on? I would have done better, it now begins to appear, to have preached the opposite doctrine of letting go—the doctrine of Socrates who called life a *peisithanatos,* a persuader of death, a teacher of the art of relinquishing. It was the doctrine of Goethe who said: *"Entsagen sollst, du sollst entsagen"*—"Thou shalt renounce." And it was the doctrine of the ancient Rabbis who despite their love of life said: "He who would die, let him hold on to life."

It is a sound doctrine.

First, because, as we have just seen, it makes peace with inevitability. And the inevitable is something with which everyone should be at peace. Second, because nothing can be more grotesque and more undignified than a futile attempt to hold on.

Let us think of the men and women who cannot grow old gracefully because they cling too hard to a youth that is escaping them; of the parents who cannot let their children go free to live their own lives; of the people who in times of general calamity have only themselves in mind.

What is it that drives people to such unseemly conduct, to such flagrant selfishness, except the attitude which I have just commended—a vigorous holding on to life? Besides, are there not times when one ought to hold life cheap, as something to be lightly surrendered? In defense of one's country, for example, in the service of truth, justice, and mercy, in the advancement of mankind?

This, then, is the great truth of human existence. One must not hold life too precious. One must always be prepared to let it go.

And now we are indeed confused. First we learn that life is a privilege—cling to it! Then we are instructed: "Thou shalt renounce!"

A paradox, and a self-contradiction! But neither the paradox nor the contradiction are of my making. They are a law written into the scheme of things—that a man must hold his existence dear and cheap at the same time.

Is it not, then, an impossible assignment to which destiny has set us? It does not ask of us that we hold life dear at one moment and cheap at the next but that we do both simultaneously. Now I can grasp something in my fist or let my hand lie open. I can clasp it to my breast or hold it at arm's length. I can embrace it, enfolding it in my arms, or let my arms hang loose. But how can I be expected to do both at once?

To which the answer is: With your body, of course not. But with your spirit, why not?

Is one not forever doing paradoxical and mutually contradictory things in his soul?

One wears his mind out in study and yet has more mind with which to study. One gives away his heart in love and yet has more heart to give away. One perishes out of pity for a suffering world and is the stronger therefore.

So, too, it is possible at one and the same time to hold on to life and let it go, provided—well, let me put it this way:

We are involved in a tug-of-war—Here on the left is the necessity to renounce life and all it contains. Here on the right, the yearning to affirm it and its experiences. And between these two is a terrible tension for they pull in opposite directions.

But suppose that here in the center I introduce a third force, one that lifts upward. My two irreconcilables now swing together, both pulling down against the new element. And the harder they pull, the closer together they come.

God is the third element, that new force that resolves the terrible contradiction, the intolerable tension of life.

And for this purpose it does not especially matter how we conceive God. I have been a great zealot for a mature idea of God. I have urged again and again that we think through our theology, not limping along on a child's notion of God as an old man in the sky. But, for my immediate purpose, all of this is irrelevant. What is relevant is this: That so soon as a man believes in God, so soon indeed as he wills to believe in Him, the terrible strain is eased; nay, it disappears, and that for two reasons.

In the first place, because a new and higher purpose is introduced into life, the purpose of doing the will of God, to put it in Jewish terms, of performing the *mitzvot.* This now becomes the reason for our existence. We are soldiers whose commander has stationed us at a post. How we like our assignment, whether we feel inclined to cling to it or to let it go, is an irrelevant issue. Our hands are too busy with our duties to be either embracing the world or pushing it away.

That is why it is written: "Make your will conform to His, then His will be yours, and all things will be as you desire."

But that, it might be urged, only evades the problem. By concentrating on duty we forget the conflicting drives within ourselves. The truth is, however, that, given God, the problem is solved not only by evasion but directly; that it is solved, curiously enough, by being made more intense. For, given God, everything becomes more precious, more to be loved and clung to, more embraceable; and yet at the same time easier to give up.

Given God, everything becomes more precious.

That sunshine in Dallas was not a chance effect, a lucky accident. It was an effect created by a great Artist, the master Painter of eternity. And because it came from God's brush it is more valuable even than I had at first conceived.

And the laughter of children, precious in itself, becomes infinitely more precious because the joy of the cosmos is in it.

And the sweetness of our friends' faces is dearer because these are fragments of an infinite sweetness.

All of life is the more treasurable because a great and holy Spirit is in it.

And yet it is easier for me to let go.

For these things are not and never have been mine. They belong to the universe and the God who stands behind it. True, I have been privileged to enjoy them for an hour, but they were always a loan due to be recalled.

And I let go of them the more easily because I know that as parts of the divine economy they will not be lost. The sunset, the bird's song, the baby's smile, the thunder of music, the surge of great poetry, the dreams of the heart, and my own being, dear to me as every man's is to him, all these I can well trust to Him who made them. There is poignancy and regret about giving them up, but no anxiety. When they slip from my hands they will pass to hands better, stronger, and wiser than mine.

This then is the insight which came to me as I stood some months ago in a blaze of sunlight: Life is dear, let us then hold it tight while we yet may; but we must hold it loosely also!

And only with God can we ease the intolerable tension of our existence. For only when He is given, can we hold life at once infinitely precious and yet as a thing lightly to be surrendered. Only because of Him is it made possible for us to clasp the world, but with relaxed hands; to embrace it, but with open arms.

Riemer, Jack, ed. *Jewish Reflections on Death.* New York: Schocken Books, Inc., 1975.

IN CONTEMPLATION OF DEATH

Lord my God and God of the universe, Creator of all that lives: although I pray for healing and continued life, still I know that I am mortal. Give me courage to accept whatever befalls me.

If only my hands were clean and my heart pure! But, alas, I have committed many wrongs and left so much undone! And yet I also know the good I did or tried to do. May that goodness impart an eternal meaning to my life.

Protector of the helpless, watch over my loved ones in whose souls my own is knit. You are my Rock and my Redeemer, the divine Source of mercy and truth.

בְּיָדוֹ אַפְקִיד רוּחִי בְּעֵת אִישַׁן וְאָעִֽירָה.
וְעִם־רוּחִי גְּוִיָּתִי; יְיָ לִי, וְלֹא אִירָא.

Beyado afkid ruchi be'et ishan vea'irah.
Ve'im ruchi geviyati; Adonai li velo ira.
Into Your hands I commend my spirit, both when I sleep and when I wake.
Body and soul are Yours, and in Your presence, Lord, I cast off fear and am at rest.

יְיָ מֶֽלֶךְ, יְיָ מָלָךְ, יְיָ יִמְלֹךְ לְעוֹלָם וָעֶד.

Adonai Melech Adonai malach Adonai yimloch le'olam va'ed.
The Lord reigns, the Lord will reign for ever and ever.

בָּרוּךְ שֵׁם כְּבוֹד מַלְכוּתוֹ לְעוֹלָם וָעֶד.

Baruch shem kevod malchuto le'olam va'ed.
Blessed is His glorious kingdom for ever and ever.

Adonai hu ha'Elohim.　　　　　　יְיָ הוּא הָאֱלֹהִים.
The Eternal Lord is God.

שְׁמַע יִשְׂרָאֵל: יְיָ אֱלֹהֵֽינוּ, יְיָ אֶחָד.

Shema Yisrael Adonai Elohenu Adonai Echad.
Hear, O Israel: the Lord is our God, the Lord is One.

AFTER DEATH

בָּרוּךְ אַתָּה, יְיָ אֱלֹהֵינוּ, מֶלֶךְ הָעוֹלָם, דַּיַּן הָאֱמֶת.

Baruch Atah Adonai Elohenu Melech ha'olam Dayan ha'emet.
Blessed is the Lord our God, Ruler of the universe, the righteous
 Judge.

Stern, Chaim, ed. *Gates of the House.* New York: Central Conference of
American Rabbis, 1976.

RECENT REFORM RESPONSA

All this applies to an apostate father. But what if the father was born a Gentile and remained a Gentile? May his Jewish son (who had converted to Judaism) say *Kaddish* for him? It is possible to take the point of view that the Jewish son should not say *Kaddish* for the gentile father. The general description in the Talmud of the relationship of a convert to his gentile relatives is that they are no longer his relatives at all. "A convert is like a newborn child" (*Yevamot* 22a), which means that entering Judaism is like a new birth and all his past life does not (legally) exist. He has no relatives any more. Of course, this general principle added to the respect in which the proselyte was held because it declared that he is not the same person who once was a pagan. Yet the principle could not be applied in the practicalities of daily life. For example, since he is newborn, then his pagan relatives are no longer his relatives. He therefore could legally now marry his sister! Yet the Talmud *(ibid.)* says that, if this were permitted, it would be said that paganism (which he had abandoned) was more sacred or moral than the Judaism he has entered.

The same situation occurs with regard to a proselyte saying *Kaddish* for his gentile father. Since by the general talmudic principle he is newborn, his gentile parents are not related to him any more, and therefore he need not say *Kaddish* for them. Indeed, this is the conclusion to which Maimonides comes (*Yad, Hilchot Avel* II: 3) and from Maimonides it is carried over to the *Shulchan Aruch* (*Yore De'ah* 374:5).

This background of the law is dealt with by Aaron Walkin, rabbi of Pinsk-Karlin, in a responsum written in 1933. He believes that, in spite of Maimonides's negative opinion mentioned above, a proselyte may say *Kaddish* for his gentile father. He calls attention to the fact that Maimonides himself (in *Hilchot Mamrin* V : 11) says that a proselyte must honor his gentile father and gives the same reason which the Talmud (in *Yevamot, ibid.*) gave as to marrying his close gentile kin, namely, that it should not be said that a proselyte has left a more sacred religion than he has entered. Therefore Rabbi Walkin concludes that, since *Kaddish* is an expression of a son's honoring his deceased father, this proselyte should say *Kaddish.*

Walkin begins by an argument a fortiori: If a son may say *Kaddish* for his Jewish-born apostate father who had willfully deserted Judaism, then certainly a proselyte son may say *Kaddish* for a gentile father who is naturally following the religion in which he was brought up.

In the responsa of Abraham Zvi Klein, rabbi in Hungary during the past century (*Birat Avraham* 11), the author is asked whether we may accept a gift for the synagogue from a gentile woman. He answers that we may do so. Then he is asked whether we may pray for her, which she had requested. To this his answer is that of course we may, and he gives the following reasons: In the Temple in Jerusalem they sacrificed seventy oxen in behalf of the seventy nations. Further, it is accepted by all Israel that the righteous of all nations have a portion in the world-to-come. In *B. Gittin* 50a, we learn that for the sake of peace we should visit the sick of Gentiles and bury their dead. When Maimonides records this law in chapter 10 of his *Hilchot Melachim,* he adds: "For the Lord is good to all and His tender mercies are over all His works." So there is no prohibition against recording her name and her good deed in the *Chevrah Kadisha,* and we should recite an *El Malei Rachamim* for her on *Yizkor* days.

Thus, while there is not very much discussion on this matter in the legal literature, yet whoever discussed the answer is in the affirmative. There may be some opinions in the negative but I have not seen them. It seems clear that, according to the law, you are completely justified (as Rabbi Teomim said) "to utter this praise of God" in honor of a deceased Christian or apostate.

Freehof, Solomon B. *Recent Reform Responsa.* Cincinnati: Hebrew Union College Press, 1963.

JEWISH EDUCATION

Resource Sheet 25

GLOSSARY

Bar/Bat (Bas) Mitzvah—

Haftarah—

Talit (Talis)—

Hebrew School—

Sunday School—

Religious School—

Cheder—

Shabbaton (pl. *Shabbatonim*)—

Kallah (pl. *Kallot*)—

Chavurah (pl. *Chavurot*)—

Ulpan (pl. *Ulpanim*)—

Resource Sheet 26

SELECTED JEWISH SOURCES

If the student is good, so is the teacher.

A village without a school should be abolished. (Talmud: *Shabbat* 119a)

The very world rests on the breath of children in the schoolhouse. (Talmud: *Shabbat* 119b)

The education of children must never be interrupted, even to rebuild the Temple. (Talmud: *Shabbat* 119b)

The person who lacks learning lacks everything.

First learn; then teach.

Learning requires a talent for sitting.

In time, even a bear can learn to dance.

Do not say: "I will learn when I will have the leisure"; you may never have it. (*Sayings of the Fathers* 2:5)

Learning is not obtained by the bashful. (*Sayings of the Fathers* 2:6)

Learning is one thing that can't be bequeathed. (*Sayings of the Fathers* 2:16)

Much have I learned from my teachers, more from my colleagues, but most from my students. (Talmud: *Ta'anit* 7b)

If you understand the shy and wherefore of what you learn, you do not forget it quickly. (Talmud: *Berachot* 5:1)

When I pray, I pray swiftly because I am talking to God; when I study, I reach slowly because God is talking to me.

—————

Leo Rosten's Treasury of Jewish Quotations, New York: McGraw-Hill, 1972.

———————————————————————

For information on *Bar/Bat Mitzvah* and confirmation, see *The Jewish Home,* Book 8.

MARRIAGE

Resource Sheet 27

GLOSSARY

Kiddushin—

Ketubah (pl. *Ketubot*)—

Chatan—

Kalah—

Chupah—

Ring—

"Harei At Mekudeshet Li"—

Shevah Berachot—

Kiddush Cup—

Glass to Break—

Yichud—

Aufruf—

Mikveh

Fasting—

Get—

Chanukat Habayit—

Mezuzah—

Klaf—

Pushke—

Kashrut—

Kosher—

Trefe—

Pareve—

Milchig—

Fleishig—

Resource Sheet 28

REFORM WEDDING SERVICE

Rabbi:

Our God and God of our fathers, bestow Your blessings upon . . . and . . . as they unite their lives in Your name. Cause them to prosper in their life together. Teach them to share life's joys and life's trials and to grow in understanding and in devotion. May love and companionship abide within the home they establish. May they grow old together in health and contentment, ever grateful unto You for the union of their lives. Amen.

Or

Heavenly Father, in this sacred hour (in the quiet of Your house), we pray for Your blessings upon these, Your children. They come to Your altar with precious gifts: (their youth) their love, their hopes and dreams, their faith in each other, and their trust in You. May they consecrate these gifts unto Your service and so find life's deepest meaning and richest happiness. Bind their lives together, O God, in sanctity and in devotion and teach them to ennoble life's experiences by sharing them in love. Amen.

בָּרוּךְ הַבָּא בְּשֵׁם יְיָ בֵּרַכְנוּכֶם מִבֵּית יְיָ.

Baruch haba beshem Adonai; berachenuchem mibet Adonai.
Blessed be he that comes in the name of the Lord; we bless you out of the house of the Lord.

עִבְדוּ אֶת־יְיָ בְּשִׂמְחָה. בֹּאוּ לְפָנָיו בִּרְנָנָה.

Ivdu et Adonai besimchah; bo'u lefanav birenanah.
Serve the Lord with gladness; come before Him with singing.

מִי אַדִּיר עַל הַכֹּל. מִי בָּרוּךְ עַל הַכֹּל. מִי גָּדוֹל עַל הַכֹּל. יְבָרֵךְ אֶת־הֶחָתָן וְאֶת־הַכַּלָּה.

Mi adir al hakol; mi baruch al hakol; mi gadol al hakol; yevarech et hechatan ve'et hakalah.
O God supremely blessed, supreme in might and glory, guide and bless this bridegroom and bride.

(Address by rabbi may be delivered here.)

(To the bridegroom): Do you . . . take . . . to be your wife, promising to cherish and protect her, whether in good fortune or in adversity, and to seek together with her a life hallowed by the faith of Israel?

(To the bride): Do you . . . take . . . to be your husband, promising to cherish and protect him, whether in good fortune or in adversity, and to seek together with him a life hallowed by the faith of Israel?

In keeping with the declaration you have made, you give and you receive this ring (these rings). It is (they are) a token of your union, a symbol of enduring loyalty. May it (they) ever remind you that your lives are to be bound together by devotion and faithfulness.

(To the bridegroom): As you . . . place this ring upon the finger of your bride, speak to her these words:

הֲרֵי אַתְּ מְקֻדֶּשֶׁת לִי בְּטַבַּעַת זוֹ כְּדָת מֹשֶׁה וְיִשְׂרָאֵל.

Harei at mekudeshet li betaba'at zo kedat Mosheh veyisrael.
With this ring be you consecrated unto me as my wife according to the law of God and the faith of Israel.

(To the bride): And you . . . (place this ring upon your bridegroom's finger as a token of wedlock and) say unto him these words:

הֲרֵי אַתָּה מְקֻדָּשׁ לִי (בְּטַבַּעַת זוֹ) כְּדָת מֹשֶׁה וְיִשְׂרָאֵל.

Harei atah mekudash li (betaba'at zo) kedat Mosheh veyisrael.
(With this ring) be you consecrated unto me as my husband according to the law of God and the faith of Israel.

Rabbi:

בָּרוּךְ אַתָּה יְיָ מְקַדֵּשׁ עַמּוֹ יִשְׂרָאֵל עַל יְדֵי (חֻפָּה וְ) קִדּוּשִׁין.

Baruch Atah Adonai mekadesh amo Yisrael al yedei (chupah ve) kiddushin.
Blessed are You, O God, who sanctify Your people Israel by the covenant of marriage.

This cup of wine is symbolic of the cup of life. As you share the one cup of wine, you undertake to share all that the future may bring. All the sweetness life's cup may hold for you should be the sweeter because you drink it together; whatever drops of bitterness it may contain should be less bitter because you share them.

As we recite the blessings over the wine, we pray that God will bestow fullness of joy upon you.

BENEDICTIONS

בָּרוּךְ אַתָּה יְיָ אֱלֹהֵינוּ מֶלֶךְ הָעוֹלָם שֶׁהַכֹּל בָּרָא לִכְבוֹדוֹ.

Baruch Atah Adonai Elohenu Melech ha'olam shehakol bara lichevodo.

Blessed are You, O Lord our God, Ruler of the universe, who have created all things for Your glory.

בָּרוּךְ אַתָּה יְיָ אֱלֹהֵינוּ מֶלֶךְ הָעוֹלָם יוֹצֵר הָאָדָם.

Baruch Atah Adonai Elohenu Melech ha'olam yotser ha'adam.

Blessed are You, O Lord our God, Ruler of the universe, Creator of man.

בָּרוּךְ אַתָּה יְיָ אֱלֹהֵינוּ מֶלֶךְ הָעוֹלָם אֲשֶׁר יָצַר אֶת־הָאָדָם בְּצַלְמוֹ. בְּצֶלֶם דְּמוּת תַּבְנִיתוֹ. וְהִתְקִין לוֹ מִמֶּנּוּ בִּנְיַן עֲדֵי עַד. בָּרוּךְ אַתָּה יְיָ יוֹצֵר הָאָדָם.

Baruch Atah Adonai Elohenu Melech ha'olam asher yatsar et ha'adam betsalmo; betselem demut tavenito; vehitkin lo mimenu binyan adei ad. Baruch Atah Adonai yotser ha'adam.

Blessed are You, O Lord our God, Ruler of the universe, who have fashioned us in Your own image and have established marriage for the fulfillment and perpetuation of life in accordance with Your holy purpose. Blessed are You, O Lord, Creator of man.

בָּרוּךְ אַתָּה יְיָ אֱלֹהֵינוּ מֶלֶךְ הָעוֹלָם אֲשֶׁר בָּרָא שָׂשׂוֹן וְשִׂמְחָה. חָתָן וְכַלָּה. גִּילָה רִנָּה. דִּיצָה וְחֶדְוָה. אַהֲבָה וְאַחֲוָה. שָׁלוֹם וְרֵעוּת. שַׂמֵּחַ תְּשַׂמַּח רֵעִים הָאֲהוּבִים. וְיִזְכּוּ לִבְנוֹת בַּיִת בְּיִשְׂרָאֵל לְשֵׁם וְלִתְהִלָּה. וִיהִי שָׁלוֹם בְּבֵיתָם וְשַׁלְוָה וְהַשֶּׁקֶט בְּלִבּוֹתָם. וְיִרְאוּ בְּנֶחָמַת יִשְׂרָאֵל וּבִתְשׁוּעַת עוֹלָם. בָּרוּךְ אַתָּה יְיָ מְשַׂמֵּחַ חָתָן עִם־הַכַּלָּה.

Baruch Atah Adonai Elohenu Melech ha'olam asher bara sason vesimchah; chatan vechalah; gilah rinah; ditsah vechedvah; ahavah ve'achavah; shalom vere'ut; same'ach tesamach re'im ha'ahuvim; veyizeku livenot bayit beyisrael leshem velithilah; vihi shalom bevetam veshalevah vehasheket belibotam; veyiru venechamat yisrael uviteshu'at olam. Baruch Atah Adonai mesame'ach chatan im hakalah.

Blessed are You, O Lord our God, Ruler of the universe, who are the Source of all gladness and joy. Through Your grace we attain affection, companionship, and peace. Grant, O Lord, that the love which unites this bridegroom and bride may grow in abiding happiness. May their family life be ennobled through their devotion to the faith of Israel. May there be peace in their home, quietness and confidence in their hearts. May they be sustained by Your comforting presence in the midst of our people and by Your promise of salvation for all mankind. Blessed are You, O Lord, who unite bridegroom and bride in holy joy. Amen.

בָּרוּךְ אַתָּה, יְיָ אֱלֹהֵינוּ, מֶלֶךְ הָעוֹלָם, בּוֹרֵא פְּרִי הַגָּפֶן.

Baruch Atah Adonai Elohenu Melech ha'olam Borei peri hagafen.
Blessed are You, O Lord our God, Ruler of the universe, Creator of the fruit of the vine.

(The wine is offered to the bridegroom and bride.)

In the presence of this company as witness you have spoken the words and performed the rites which unite your lives. I, therefore, declare you . . . and . . . husband and wife; married in accordance with the laws of the State of . . . and according to the tradition of our Jewish faith.

And now I ask you and all your dear ones to bow your heads in reverence. Silently let us pray that God will bless your home and help you to achieve your highest hopes.

(Pause for silent prayer.)

יְבָרֶכְךָ יְיָ וְיִשְׁמְרֶךָ,

יָאֵר יְיָ פָּנָיו אֵלֶיךָ וִיחֻנֶּךָּ,

יִשָּׂא יְיָ פָּנָיו אֵלֶיךָ וְיָשֵׂם לְךָ שָׁלוֹם.

Yevarechecha Adonai veyishmerecha
Ya'er Adonai panav elecha vichuneka
Yisa Adonai panav elecha veyasem lecha shalom.
May the Lord bless you and keep you
May the Lord cause His countenance to shine upon you and be
    gracious unto you
May the Lord lift up His countenance unto you and give you peace.
    Amen.

Rabbi's Manual. New York: Central Conference of American Rabbis, 1961.

Resource Sheet 29

WEDDING SONGSHEET

SIMAN TOV

Siman tov umazal tov, umazal tov vesiman tov (3x)
Yehei lanu
Yehei lanu, yehei lanu, ulechol am Yisrael. (4x)
(A good sign and good luck—for us and for the entire people of
    Israel.)

OD YISHAMA

Od yishama be'arei Yehudah uvechutzot Yerushalayim (2x)
Kol sason vekol simchah, kol chatan vekol kalah. (2x)
(May there always be heard in the cities of Judah and in the streets
    of Jerusalem the voice of gladness and the voice of joy, the voice
    of the bridegroom and the voice of the bride.)

Resource Sheet 30

SEX IS FOR WOMEN TOO

The Bible catalogues three primary obligations of husbands to wives: food, clothing, and sexual rights. The Talmud then singles out sexual rights as the most important of these by stipulating that a woman may, by prenuptial agreement, surrender her right to food and clothing—but never to sexual gratification! The famous schools of Shammai and Hillel disagreed on how long a man could deny sexual intercourse to his wife before she would be entitled to ask for a divorce. According to the former, two weeks; according to the latter, only one.

Perhaps the most amazing aspect of these statements is that they were issued—all of them—by men addressing themselves to other men. At a time when, among other peoples, women were valued only as receptacles for male gratification and impregnation, Judaism revealed a most astonishing sensitivity to the fact that women possessed active sexual needs.

Men were even obliged by our tradition to anticipate the sexual moods of their wives, to initiate intercourse when it was reasonable to suppose a feminine desire for it. They were instructed, moreover, to increase a woman's sexual pleasure by commencing with exciting foreplay. The following remarkable instruction is from a thirteenth-century marriage manual, *Iggeret Hakodesh*, usually attributed to Nachmanides, though the authorship is not entirely certain:

> . . . Engage her first in conversation that puts her heart and mind at ease and gladdens her. . . . Speak words which arouse her to passion, union, love, desire, and eros—and words which elicit attitudes of reverence for God, piety, and modesty. Tell her of pious and good women who gave birth to fine and pure children. . . . Speak with her words, some of love, some of erotic passion, some of piety and reverence. . . . Hurry not to arouse passion until her mood is ready; begin in love; let her orgasm take place first. . . .

Quite obviously, in addition to the most admirable kind of sensitivity, the Rabbis were aware of some of the physiological differences between men and women. . . .

They were curious, as we are, as to what caused a fetus to be conceived as male or female. Granting the sexism of their preference for boys, it is deeply significant that they said: When the woman experiences her orgasm first, a son results; if the husband comes first, it will be a daughter. In short, if a man wanted a son, he had better attend to the sexual needs of his wife!

The teachings of some religions in regard to sex make it very difficult for young people in those denominations to cope with their own feelings of sexual desire. Adolescence, after all, is a time of increasing sexual interest. It marks the emergence of a person from childhood into adulthood—the time when all the organs and glands of the body are ripening for full use in marriage. At such a time it would be unnatural for any of us not to feel a strong physical attraction for the opposite sex. To tell a young person that it is wrong to feel what nature itself impels one to feel is to create an almost intolerable problem.

Judaism helps us face this difficult but wonderful period of life in a wholesome way. It tells us we should not feel guilty over our strong feelings of sexual desire; if God did not want us to experience such sensations, He would have created us differently. Judaism teaches that life is good and sex is good—if we accept it and learn how to control and use it for our advantage and richest growth.

Clearly, then, there has been major disagreement between Judaism and Christianity regarding sex. The fact that today the difference is less than it once was is a tribute to the ancient insight of our tradition. It would be dishonest to pretend that every Jew in the world knows or follows the traditional attitude of our faith toward sex. Those who do, however, can live a healthier, more wholesome life, with greater probability of happiness in their marriages.

Here are a few of the injunctions which our rabbinic forebears promulgated:

Your wife has been given to you in order that you may realize with her life's great plan; she is not yours to vex or grieve. Vex her not, for God notes her tears.

A wife is the joy of man's heart.

A man should eat less than he can afford and should honor his wife and children more than he can afford.

A man should be careful not to irritate his wife and cause her to weep.

If your wife is short, bend down and whisper to her.

He who loves his wife as himself, who honors her more than himself, who rears his children in the right path, and who marries them off at the proper time of their life, concerning him it is written: And you will know that your home is peace.

Man should ever be mindful of the honor of his wife for she is responsible for all the blessings found in his household.

A man must not cause his wife to weep for God counts her tears.

Strive to fulfill your wife's wishes for it is equivalent to doing God's will.

How can we account for the fact that all these instructions are directed to the husband? Does this mean only he must act considerately in order for the marriage to succeed? How about the wife's meeting his needs? Does a weeping wife always mean a bad marriage? Why does one of these quotations stipulate that a man should love his wife "as himself"? Should he not love her more than himself? What do you think of this same statement's apparent implication that a man should honor his wife even more than he loves her?

The following additional rabbinic comments may help you answer some of these questions:

When the husband is blessed, his wife is also blessed thereby.

A wife who receives love gives love in return; if she receives anger, she returns anger in equal measure.

In the same category is the talmudic dictum that the choice of a new place of residence or of a different profession must be made jointly by husband and wife. Significantly enough, the only circumstance in which this did not hold was if one of them wished to live in the Holy Land and the other did not. In that event, the desire of the one who wanted to live in the land of Israel received priority.

Finally, Jewish tradition has long recognized that husband and wife must be sensitive to each other's moods and needs, must be able to perceive them, even without a word from the other.

Thus a chasidic rabbi related this incident:

> A commander-in-chief received a message telling him that his main line of defense had been broken by the enemy. He was greatly distressed and his emotions showed plainly on his countenance. His wife heard the nature of the message and, entering her husband's room, she said: "I too at this very moment have received tidings worse than yours."
>
> "And what are they?" inquired the commander with agitation.
>
> "I have read discouragement on your face," replied the wife. "Loss of courage is worse than loss of defense."

The teachings of Judaism about marriage have not been just theoretical. That they have actually influenced behavior is indicated by studies which reveal that among Jews in the United States marriages occur at a later age than in other groups and that Jews are likely to have more stable marriages than others.

Gittelsohn, Roland B. *Love, Sex, and Marriage: A Jewish View.* New York: Union of American Hebrew Congregations, 1980.

Resource Sheet 31

THE PROCEDURE FOR DIVORCE

The following is the Jewish divorce procedure based on the *Seder Haget* given at the end of chapter 154 of *Even Haezer* (the part of the *Shulchan Aruch* concerned with marriage and divorce). The English text was prepared by the late Professor Boaz Cohen ז״ל.

Rabbi (to husband): Do you Ploni ben Ploni [so-and-so, the son of so-and-so] give this *get* of your own free will without duress and compulsion?

Husband: Yes.

Rabbi: Perhaps you have bound yourself by uttering a vow or by making any binding statement which would compel you to give a *get* against your will?

Husband: No.

Rabbi: Perhaps you have once made a statement which would invalidate the *get,* or you have uttered or done something to render the *get* null and void and have forgotten it, or you were under the erroneous impression that such acts do not render the *get* null and void; will you therefore please make void all such remarks and acts of yours in the presence of witnesses?

Husband: Hear you witnesses; in your presence I declare null and void any previous declaration that I may have made which may invalidate this *get.* I also declare any witness that may hereafter testify to such a statement as disqualified.

Sofer [a scribe] (to husband): You, Ploni ben Ploni, I am presenting to you as a gift these writing materials, the paper, the pen, and the ink so that they become your property.

(Husband accepts the writing materials, lifts them up to show that he has acquired them.)

Husband: You witnesses, listen to what I will say to the *sofer.* (Then, addressing the *sofer,* he says:) You, *sofer,* Ploni ben Ploni, I give you this paper, ink, pen, and all the writing materials and I order you that you write for me, Ploni ben Ploni, a *get* to divorce my wife, Plonit bat Ploni, and write this *get lishmi, lishmah, uleshem gerushin* [for me exclusively, for her exclusively, and for the purpose of a *get* exclusively], and write even as many as a hundred *gittin,* if necessary, until one valid *get* is written and signed according to the law of Moses and the Children of Israel. I hereby authorize you to make any corrections in the document that may be necessary.

Sofer: So I shall do.

Husband (to each witness in the hearing of the other): You, Ploni ben Ploni, act as witness and sign the *get* which the *sofer,* Ploni ben Ploni, shall write specifically for me, Ploni ben Ploni, and for my wife, Plonit bat Ploni, and sign as many as a hundred *gittin* if necessary until one valid *get* is written and signed and delivered according to the law of Moses and the Children of Israel.

Each witness: So I shall do.

(Husband then hands over the writing material to the *sofer.*)

Sofer (to witnesses): Hear you witnesses: All these preparations that I make and all the writing that I shall do, I shall do in the name of the husband, Ploni ben Ploni, to divorce his wife, Plonit bat Ploni, and I am writing it *lishmo, lishmah, uleshem gerushin.*

The *get* is then written and the witnesses must be present during the writing of the first line. The witnesses, as well as the scribe, make a distinguishing mark on the *get.* When the *get* is finished and the ink is dried, the witnesses read the *get.*

(Before the witnesses sign it, they say to each other): You, Ploni ben Ploni, witness that I am signing this *get leshem* [in the name of] Ploni ben Ploni, who ordered us to sign a *get* to divorce his wife, Plonit bat Ploni, and I am signing it *lishmo, lishmah, uleshem gerushin.*

Rabbi (to *sofer*): You, *sofer,* Ploni ben Ploni, is this the *get* that you have written?

Sofer: Yes.

Rabbi: Do you have any special mark by which you can identify this *get?*

Sofer: Yes and this is it (points it out).

Rabbi: Did Ploni ben Ploni give you the writing materials in the presence of the witnesses?

Sofer: Yes.

Rabbi: Did the husband tell you to write the *get?*

Sofer: Yes.

Rabbi: Did he tell you to write it *lishmo, lishmah, uleshem gerushin?*

Sofer: Yes.

Rabbi: Did he order you in the presence of witnesses?

Sofer: Yes.

Rabbi: Did you write it *lishmo, lishmah, uleshem gerushin?*

Sofer: Yes.

Rabbi: What did you say before you started writing this *get?*

Sofer: I said: "I write this *get* in the name of the husband, Ploni ben Ploni, to divorce with it his wife, Plonit bat Ploni, and I write it *lishmo, lishmah, uleshem gerushin.* "

Rabbi: Did you say so in the presence of witnesses?

Sofer: Yes.

Rabbi: Were the witnesses present at least during the time you wrote the first line?

Sofer: Yes.

Rabbi (to witnesses): Did you, witnesses, hear the husband, Ploni ben Ploni, order the *sofer* to write a *get* for his wife, Ploni bat Ploni, and to write it *lishmo, lishmah, uleshem gerushin?*

Witnesses: We did.

Rabbi: Were you present when he wrote the first line?

Witnesses: We were.

Rabbi (to each witness separately): Is this your signature?

Each witness: Yes.

Rabbi: Did you sign it *lishmo, lishmah, uleshem gerushin?*

Each witness: Yes.

Rabbi: Did the husband tell you to do so?

Each witness: Yes.

Rabbi: Did the other witness see you sign the *get?*

Witness: Yes.

Rabbi: What did you say before you signed?

Witness: I said: "I am signing this *get* in the name of the husband, Ploni ben Ploni, to divorce with it his wife, Plonit bat Ploni, and I am signing it *lishmo, lishmah, uleshem gerushin.*" So I said and so I signed.

(Rabbi repeats this with second witness. Then the *get* is read again to check that it is correct.)

Rabbi (to husband): Again I wish to ask you whether you give this *get* of your own free will.

Husband: I do.

Rabbi: Did you bind yourself by any statement or by any vow in a way that would compel you to give this *get* against your free will?

Husband: No.

Rabbi: Again I wish to ask you that perhaps you did make such a statement and have forgotten it or made it erroneously. Will you therefore cancel all such statements and declare them null and void?

Husband: You witnesses hear that I declare in your presence null and void all previous declarations that I have made which may invalidate this *get*. I also declare any witness that may testify to such a statement as disqualified.

Rabbi (to wife): Are you accepting this *get* of your own free will?

Wife: Yes.

Rabbi: Did you bind yourself by any statement or vow that would compel you to accept this *get* against your will?

Wife: No.

Rabbi: Perhaps you have unwittingly made such a statement that would nullify the *get*. In order to prevent that, will you kindly retract all such declarations?

Wife: I revoke all such statements that may nullify the *get,* in the presence of you the witnesses.

Rabbi (to those present): If there is anyone who wishes to protest let him do so now.

Husband (to witnesses): You be also witnesses to the delivery of the *get*.

(Rabbi now tells the wife to remove all jewelry from her hands, to hold her hands together with open palms upward to receive the *get*. The *sofer* holds the *get* and gives it to the rabbi. The rabbi gives the *get* to the husband who, holding it in both hands, drops it into the palms of the wife and says:) This be your *get* and with it be you divorced from this time forth so that you may become the wife of any man.

(The wife receives the *get,* lifts up her hands, walks with it a short distance, and returns. She returns the *get* to the rabbi. The rabbi reads the *get* again with the witnesses. The rabbi again asks the *sofer* and witnesses to identify the *get* and the signatures.)

Rabbi: Hear all you present that Rabbenu Tam has issued a ban against all those who try to invalidate a *get* after it has been delivered.

The four corners of the *get* are then cut and it is placed in the files of the rabbi. The husband and the wife receive written statements called *petur,* which certify that their marriage has been dissolved according to the requirements of Jewish law.

1. There is great stress that the *get* be written *lishmah,* that is, with the particular man and woman in mind. If this is not done, the *get* is not valid. The requirement that the *get* be written *lishmah* is derived by the talmudic authorities from the words in the verse from Deuteronomy (24:1), *"vekatav lah"*—he writes her a bill of divorcement, meaning it is *only* for her.

2. Furthermore, as is obvious from the verse in Deuteronomy, the obligation is on the husband to write the *get* himself. Because we now have scribes who are specially trained in the technical aspects of writing the document, the husband must turn over his obligation to the scribe. For that reason he must formally acquire the materials (usually as a gift from the *sofer*) with which the *get* is prepared and then legally give them to the scribe, so that the scribe can serve as his agent in preparing the document.

3. The *get* must be conveyed from the husband to the wife, and she must indicate her possession of it by lifting her hands, etc. This is in fulfillment of the requirement that there be a valid *kinyan*— means of conveyance and acquisition.

4. The wife removes her finger jewelry before receiving the *get* so that nothing comes between the document and her whole hands' acceptance of it.

5. The "distinguishing mark" on the *get* is made so that, if the validity of the *get* is later challenged, the *sofer* will be able, by checking for the distinguishing mark, to ascertain that it is indeed the document he prepared. For example, he might arrange the lettering of the *get* so that the last letter of the last three lines of the document will, if read down, spell אמן , amen.

6. The document is cut at the very end of the divorce so that it can never be reused fraudulently by any other party.

[While it is true that the ceremony is archaic in nature, the strong stamp of ritual adds to the solemnity of the occasion and creates a deep feeling of tradition. The halachic reasons for some of the procedures are complicated. This whole procedure, including the writing of the *get,* usually takes no more than two hours and requires only a few participants—the couple, the rabbi, the witnesses, and the *sofer.*]

Strassfeld, Michael, and Strassfeld, Sharon, compilers and eds. *The Second Jewish Catalog.* Philadelphia: The Jewish Publication Society of America, 1976.

Resource Sheet 32

CONSECRATION OF A HOUSE

For the ceremony of consecration, a *mezuzah,* a Bible, wine, *chalah,* and salt are required. Members of the household and guests participate in reading the ritual.

In the spirit of our Jewish faith, we consecrate this house with prayers of thanksgiving and invoke upon it the blessing of God.

שְׁמַע יִשְׂרָאֵל: יְיָ אֱלֹהֵינוּ, יְיָ אֶחָד.

Shema Yisrael Adonai Elohenu Adonai Echad.
Hear, O Israel: the Lord is our God, the Lord is One.

בָּרוּךְ שֵׁם כְּבוֹד מַלְכוּתוֹ לְעוֹלָם וָעֶד.

Baruch shem kevod malchuto le'olam va'ed.
Blessed is His glorious kingdom for ever and ever.

וְאָהַבְתָּ אֵת יְיָ אֱלֹהֶיךָ בְּכָל־לְבָבְךָ וּבְכָל־נַפְשְׁךָ וּבְכָל־מְאֹדֶךָ.
וְהָיוּ הַדְּבָרִים הָאֵלֶּה, אֲשֶׁר אָנֹכִי מְצַוְּךָ הַיּוֹם, עַל־לְבָבֶךָ.
וְשִׁנַּנְתָּם לְבָנֶיךָ, וְדִבַּרְתָּ בָּם בְּשִׁבְתְּךָ בְּבֵיתֶךָ, וּבְלֶכְתְּךָ
בַדֶּרֶךְ, וּבְשָׁכְבְּךָ וּבְקוּמֶךָ.

Ve'ahavta et Adonai Elohecha bechol levavecha uvechol nafshecha uvechol me'odecha. Vehayu hadevarim ha'eleh asher Anochi metsavecha hayom al levavecha. Veshinantam levanecha vedibarta bam beshivtecha bevetecha uvelechtecha vaderech uveshochbecha uvekumecha.

You shall love the Lord your God with all your mind, with all your strength, with all your being. Set these words, which I command you this day, upon your heart. Teach them faithfully to your children; speak of them in your home and on your way, when you lie down and when you rise up.

וּקְשַׁרְתָּם לְאוֹת עַל־יָדֶךָ, וְהָיוּ לְטֹטָפֹת בֵּין עֵינֶיךָ, וּכְתַבְתָּם
עַל־מְזֻזוֹת בֵּיתֶךָ, וּבִשְׁעָרֶיךָ.

Ukeshartam le'ot al yadecha vehayu letotafot ben enecha uchetavtam al mezuzot betecha uvisharecha.

Bind them as a sign upon your hand; let them be a symbol before your eyes; inscribe them on the doorposts of your house, and on your gates.

לְמַעַן תִּזְכְּרוּ וַעֲשִׂיתֶם אֶת־כָּל־מִצְוֹתָי, וִהְיִיתֶם קְדֹשִׁים
לֵאלֹהֵיכֶם. אֲנִי יְיָ אֱלֹהֵיכֶם, אֲשֶׁר הוֹצֵאתִי אֶתְכֶם מֵאֶרֶץ
מִצְרַיִם לִהְיוֹת לָכֶם לֵאלֹהִים. אֲנִי יְיָ אֱלֹהֵיכֶם.

Lema'an tizkeru va'asitem et kol mitsvotai viheyitem kedoshim lelohechem. Ani Adonai Elohechem asher hotseti etechem me'eretz Mitsrayim liheyot lachem lelohim; Ani Adonai Elohechem.
Be mindful of all My *mitzvot,* and do them: so shall you consecrate yourselves to your God. I, the Lord, am your God who led you out of Egypt to be your God; I, the Lord, am your God.

Our homes have always been the dwelling place of the Jewish spirit. Our tables have been altars of faith and love. "When words of Torah pass between us, the Divine Presence is in our midst." Our doors have been open to the stranger and the needy. May this home we now consecrate keep alive the beauty of our noble heritage.

(*Chalah* is dipped in salt and distributed.)

בָּרוּךְ אַתָּה, יְיָ אֱלֹהֵינוּ, מֶלֶךְ הָעוֹלָם, הַמּוֹצִיא לֶחֶם מִן
הָאָרֶץ.

Baruch Atah Adonai Elohenu Melech ha'olam hamotzi lechem min ha'aretz.
Blessed is the Lord our God, Ruler of the universe, who causes bread to come forth from the earth.

(Wine is given to each guest.)

Wine is a symbol of joy. May all who dwell within these walls, and all who enter here, know contentment, happiness, and peace.

בָּרוּךְ אַתָּה, יְיָ אֱלֹהֵינוּ, מֶלֶךְ הָעוֹלָם, בּוֹרֵא פְּרִי הַגָּפֶן.

Baruch Atah Adonai Elohenu Melech ha'olam Borei peri hagafen.
Blessed is the Lord our God, Ruler of the universe, Creator of the fruit of the vine.

(The open Bible is raised.)

The Torah has been our life; it has taught us how to live. May this home be a place for learning and doing. May the hearts of all who dwell here be filled with a love of the Torah and its teachings.

בָּרוּךְ אַתָּה, יְיָ אֱלֹהֵינוּ, מֶלֶךְ הָעוֹלָם, אֲשֶׁר קִדְּשָׁנוּ בְּמִצְוֹתָיו וְצִוָּנוּ לַעֲסוֹק בְּדִבְרֵי תוֹרָה.

Baruch Atah Adonai Elohenu Melech ha'olam asher kideshanu be-mitsvotav vetsivanu la'asok bediverei Torah.

Blessed is the Lord our God, Ruler of the universe, by whose *mitzvot* we are hallowed, who commands us to engage in the study of Torah.

PSALM 15

יְיָ, מִי־יָגוּר בְּאָהֳלֶךָ, מִי־יִשְׁכֹּן בְּהַר קָדְשֶׁךָ? הוֹלֵךְ תָּמִים וּפֹעֵל צֶדֶק וְדֹבֵר אֱמֶת בִּלְבָבוֹ.

Adonai mi yagur be' oholecha mi yishkon behar kodeshecha?
Holech tamim ufo'el tsedek vedover emet bilevavo.

Lord, who may abide in Your house? Who may dwell in Your holy mountain?

Those who are upright; who do justly; who speak the truth within their hearts.

לֹא־רָגַל עַל־לְשֹׁנוֹ, לֹא־עָשָׂה לְרֵעֵהוּ רָעָה, וְחֶרְפָּה לֹא־נָשָׂא עַל־קְרֹבוֹ. נִבְזֶה בְּעֵינָיו נִמְאָס, וְאֶת־יִרְאֵי יְיָ יְכַבֵּד.

Lo ragal al leshono lo asah lere'ehu ra'ah vecherepah lo nasa al kerovo.
Nivezeh ve'enav nimas ve'et yirei Adonai yechabed.

Who do not slander others, or wrong them, or bring shame upon them.

Who scorn the lawless, but honor those who revere the Lord.

נִשְׁבַּע לְהָרַע וְלֹא יָמִיר, כַּסְפּוֹ לֹא־נָתַן בְּנֶשֶׁךְ וְשֹׁחַד עַל־נָקִי לֹא־לָקָח.

Nishba lehara velo yamir
kaspo lo natan beneshech veshochad al naki lo lakach.

Who give their word, and, come what may, do not retract.
Who do not exploit others, who never take bribes.

Oseh eleh lo yimot le'olam. עֹשֶׂה אֵלֶּה לֹא יִמּוֹט לְעוֹלָם.
Those who live in this way shall never be shaken.

(An additional scriptural passage, such as First Kings 8:54–61, might be read here.)

(The *mezuzah* is raised.)

This ancient symbol speaks to us of our need to love God and to live by the words of the Eternal One. We affix the *mezuzah* to the doorposts of this house with the hope that it will always remind us of our duties to God and to one another. May the Divine Spirit fill this house—the spirit of love and kindness and consideration for all people.

בָּרוּךְ אַתָּה, יְיָ אֱלֹהֵינוּ, מֶלֶךְ הָעוֹלָם, אֲשֶׁר קִדְּשָׁנוּ בְּמִצְוֹתָיו וְצִוָּנוּ לִקְבּוֹעַ מְזוּזָה.

Baruch Atah Adonai Elohenu Melech ha'olam asher kideshanu be-mitsvotav vetsivanu likebo'a mezuzah.
Blessed is the Lord our God, Ruler of the universe, by whose *mitzvot* we are hallowed, who commands us to affix the *mezuzah*.

(The *mezuzah,* its top inclining inward, is affixed to the upper part of the doorpost on the right, as one enters the house. If desired, a *mezuzah* may be affixed to the right doorpost of the principal rooms.)

בָּרוּךְ אַתָּה, יְיָ אֱלֹהֵינוּ, מֶלֶךְ הָעוֹלָם, שֶׁהֶחֱיָנוּ וְקִיְּמָנוּ וְהִגִּיעָנוּ לַזְּמַן הַזֶּה.

Baruch Atah Adonai Elohenu Melech ha'olam shehecheyanu vekiyemanu vehigianu lazeman hazeh.
Blessed is the Lord our God, Ruler of the universe, for giving us life, for sustaining us, and for enabling us to reach this happy day.

אִם־יְיָ לֹא יִבְנֶה בַיִת, שָׁוְא עָמְלוּ בוֹנָיו בּוֹ.

Im Adonai lo yiveneh vayit shav amelu vonav bo.
Unless the Lord builds the house, its builders toil in vain.

In this awareness we pray that our home be blessed by the sense of God's presence.

Accept, O God, our offering of thanksgiving for the promise of security and happiness this home represents, and fortify our resolve to make it, now and always, a temple dedicated to you. Let it be filled with the beauty of holiness and the warmth of love. May the guest and stranger find within it welcome and friendship. So will it ever merit the praise: "How lovely are your tents, O Jacob, your dwelling-places, O Israel!"

For all who are assembled here, and for all who will enter these doors, we invoke Your blessing:

יְיָ יִשְׁמָר־צֵאתְךָ וּבוֹאֶךָ, מֵעַתָּה וְעַד־עוֹלָם.

Adonai yishmor tsetecha uvo'echa me'atah ve'ad olam.

May the Lord watch over you when you go out and when you come in, now and always. Amen.

Stern, Chaim, ed. *Gates of the House.* New York: Central Conference of American Rabbis, 1976.

Resource Sheet 33

ON THE SEVEN WEDDING BLESSINGS

by Herbert Bronstein

Traditional Jewish worship was designed around the three overarching biblical motifs of Creation, Redemption (Exodus), and Revelation (Sinai). The entire round of Jewish observance is suffused by these same three themes. Thus, in the holiday cycle, *Rosh Hashanah* is clearly associated with Creation; *Pesach* with Exodus; *Shavuot* with Sinai. For *Kiddushin,* the act of marriage, the Rabbis of our classic period chose the theme of Creation around which to design the celebratory blessings. These are known in our tradition as the *Sheva Berachot,* the Seven Blessings of Praise.

Indeed the *Sheva Berachot* contain in brief compass the entire sweep of the Jewish conception of existence, from the miraculous glory of the original panoply of Creation to the sublime perfection of Creation in the messianic completion. Both the evocation of Paradise and the affirmation of the messianic celebration are comprised in a seven-versed poem on the theme of Creation, which bears the luster of that crystallization which is the mark of poetry of genius. Even the *number* of blessings, *seven,* which is the numerical symbol of the cosmos, emblematic of the seven days of Creation, of the spheres, of light (the *menorah*), is meant to convey the unified theme of Creation.

Of the three major motifs of biblical Judaism, why did the Rabbis choose the theme of Creation for the blessings of *Kiddushin?* Undoubtedly, first, because the miracle of Creation is renewed in procreation. Out of the very substance and spirit of husband and wife, created in the image of God, is spun the perpetual, miraculous fabric of life. Also, for the couple, a new life, a new world, does, in marriage, come into being. That is why, in the Jewish folkloristic conception, husband and wife are as newborn in marriage; they are, as it were, sinless, blessed with a whole new start in life.

Further, the purpose of Jewish existence is the partnership with God in the maintenance, the harmonization, of Creation. And every good marriage is considered to be a *tikkun,* a "putting in order," for each good marriage lifts existence to a state of higher harmony.

Within the tradition, especially among the mystics, can be found the idea that every true act of love in marriage is itself a *tikkun* uniting the transcendent and immanent aspects of Divinity, an analogy to spiritual and physical union in married love.

Thus, the consecration of a marriage is a cause for great rejoicing. Of all relationships, the marriage relationship is *kodesh kodashim*— the holy of holies—and the wedding, among all the rejoicings of life, is the *simchat semachot*—the celebration of celebrations. Indeed, in traditional Jewish life, the union of two lives was the occasion for celebration by the entire community. It is as if the framers of the wedding service gathered from the garden of the Hebrew language a whole cluster of words signifying happiness and joy and put them together in the blessings, like a floral bouquet for bride and groom: "Joy and gladness, mirth and exultation, pleasure and delight. . . ." And again: "We praise You, O God, who bring joy to bridegroom and bride." And again: "And make the bridegroom greatly to rejoice with his bride even as You gladdened Your first creatures in Eden. . . ."

And yet, while certainly expressing an ethos of pleasure in life, the *Sheva Berachot* do not encourage the couple to relinquish social obligations or, through self-isolating privatism, to endeavor escape from the ills of the world. The text of the blessings also evokes the messianic hope. The couple are encouraged to look beyond their private Eden toward the vision of Zion rejoicing with *all* her children. In the reference toward the end of the blessings to Jeremiah's vision (33:10–11), which sees beyond the terrors of the world to the ultimate wedding celebration in the peace of Zion, the couple are reminded of the Jewish commitment to the work of redemption for all.

As the couple begin to create their own world, they know that together they must bring something to the perfection of God's Creation, so that the time may soon come when God, as it were, will rejoice with His bride, the people of Israel.

Maslin, Simeon J., ed. *Gates of Mitzvah.* New York: Central Conference of American Rabbis, 1979.

For further information on the Jewish wedding, see *The Jewish Home,* Books 9 and 10.

PESACH

Resource Sheet 34

GLOSSARY

Pesach—

Seder—

Haggadah (pl. *Haggadot*)—

Matzah—

Chamets—

The Four Cups—

The Four Questions—

The Cup of Elijah—

Karpas—

Maror—

Charoset—

Shankbone—

Egg—

Afikoman—

Opening the Door—

Ma'ot Chitim—

Shabbat Hagadol—

SCHEMA OF THE SEDER

1. Light the holiday candles.
2. First cup of wine is filled.
   a. *Kadesh* (sanctification) = "... *Borei peri hagafen*" + "*Shehe-cheyanu.*"
   b. Drink wine.
3. *Urechats* (ceremonial washing of hands, without a blessing).
4. *Karpas* (greens).
   a. Say "... *Borei peri ha'adamah.*"
   b. Eat greens.
5. *Yachats* (breaking of the *matzah*).
   a. Break middle *matzah,* hiding half as the *afikoman* to be eaten after meal.
   b. Say "*Ha lachma anya. . . .*"
6. *Magid* (recitation of the service).
   a. The Four Questions.
   b. *Avadim Hayinu.*
   c. The Four Children.
   d. The Ten Plagues.
   e. *Dayenu.*
   f. Pointing out the *Pesach* symbols.
   g. *Hallel* (Psalms of Praise).
   h. Drink second cup ("... *Borei peri hagafen*").
7. *Rachtsah* (washing of hands).
   Recite blessing "... *Al netilat yadayim.*"
8. *Motzi, matzah.*
   a. Say "... *Hamotzi* ..." + "... *Al achilat matzah.*"
   b. Eat *matzah.*
9. *Maror.*
   a. Say "... *Al achilat maror.*"
   b. Eat bitter herb dipped in *charoset.*
10. *Korech* (reminder of the Temple).
    Bottom *matzah* broken and eaten with horseradish (and *charoset*).
11. *Shulchan Orech* (the *Pesach* meal).
12. *Tsafun* (eating the *afikoman*).

13. *Barech* (grace after meal).
   a. Fill cups for third time and say *"Birkat Hamazon."*
   b. Say *". . . Borei peri hagafen"* and drink third cup.
   c. Open door and sing *"Eliyahu Hanavi."*
14. *Hallel.*
   a. Say final benedictions.
   b. Say *". . . Borei peri hagafen"* and drink fourth cup.
15. *Nirtsah* (conclusion).
16. Sing songs.
   a. *"Echad Mi Yodea?"* (Who Knows One?)
   b. Others.

Resource Sheet 36

PREPARATION FOR PASSOVER

There are many levels of Passover observance within the Jewish community. The spectrum ranges from those Jews who simply refrain from eating leavened bread to those who use utensils and dishes completely different from those used during the rest of the year. Reform Jews are encouraged to find that level of observance which is meaningful to them and which enhances their celebration of the festival.

The following represents a scrupulous level of preparation. Students should not approach this with an "all-or-nothing" attitude. This material is presented to allow the students a full range of options as they explore their own observance of the holiday.

DISHES AND UTENSILS

1. Only dishes and utensils specially reserved for Passover are used, with the following exceptions:
    a. Silverware, knives, forks, and spoons made wholly of metal, if used during the year, may be used on Passover if thoroughly scoured and immersed in boiling water. All table glassware is permitted after thorough scouring.
    b. Metal pots and pans used for cooking purposes only, but not for baking, if made wholly of metal, though used during the year, may be used on Passover if first thoroughly scoured and immersed in boiling water.

Note: Utensils used for baking during the year are not used during Passover.

2. Earthenware, enamelware, and porcelain utensils used during the year are not used on *Pesach.*

3. The stove is prepared for *Pesach* by thoroughly scrubbing and cleansing all parts and turning full flame on in the bake oven and all the grates.

4. A dishwashing machine may be used for Passover after thorough scouring with boiling water and the use of a new tray.

FOOD

1. Not permitted *(chamets):*
The following foods are forbidden during *Pesach:* leavened bread, cakes, biscuits and crackers, cereals, coffee substances derived from cereals, wheat, barley, oats, rice, peas, corn, and all liquids which contain ingredients or flavors made from grain alcohol.

2. Permitted foods:
   a. Requiring no "kosher for Passover" label but must be in unopened packages or containers: natural coffee, sugar, tea, salt, pepper, vegetables except peas and beans (but string beans are permitted).
   b. Frozen fruits and vegetables. Fruits and those vegetables normally permitted for Passover use are permitted in their frozen state.
   c. If certified for Passover use by rabbinical authority: *matzah, matzah* flour, Passover noodles, candies, cakes, beverages, canned and processed foods, milk, butter, cheese, jams, jellies, vinegar, wines and liquors, vegetable gelatins, relishes, salad oils, dried fruits, shortening.

YOU CAN AND SHOULD CONDUCT A SEDER

Don't say you can't conduct a *seder*. You can!

To conduct a *seder* is not as hard as you think, or as complicated, and you will gain great satisfaction.

It would be a pity if Passover were to pass over your home without the home observance which enables you to relive the fight for liberty experienced by our ancestors and without the ceremony which strengthens the bond between all Jews.

Here are some tips which will help you make your *seder* successful:

1. Make sure everyone has the same *haggadah*. It is fine for two people to share a *haggadah*. There are many beautiful *haggadot* now on the market and you have a wide choice.

2. Don't feel that your *seder* must be too formal. You may interpolate into the various parts of the service your own comments. You may ask others to do the same. Keep the service moving along, but don't feel that it has quite the same formality as a synagogue service. The *seder* is a unique admixture of the solemn and the joyful.

3. Study the *haggadah* before the night of the *seder*. Decide in advance which parts you can do in Hebrew and which in English. Be familiar with the text before you sit down for the ceremony.

4. Rotate the reading of the parts of the *haggadah* among those at the table. Some will read in English; others in Hebrew. Some will sing the songs in one style; others will use another melody. The very melange of the Hebrew dialects and the variations in the manner of reading portions of the service will illustrate the diversity of Jewish life and add a special flavor to the proceedings.

5. Have the guests recite as many of the blessings as possible in unison. Some segments can be read in unison so as to encourage the participation of everyone.

Traditionally, Passover is a time when you can derive both merriment and inspiration from the great saga of the Exodus. Don't lose the opportunity of introducing the Passover spirit into your own home. You will feel amply rewarded for the little effort entailed.

Resource Sheet 38

THE MATZAH OF HOPE

Note that a fourth *matzah* should be placed on the ceremonial tray. Immediately before *Hamotzi,* the leader sets aside this *matzah* and says:

THIS IS THE *"MATZAH* OF HOPE."

This *matzah,* which we set aside as a symbol of hope for the Jews suffering oppression in the Soviet Union, Ethiopia, and in Moslem lands. . . .

Our Father in heaven, on this watchnight of the Passover festival, we gratefully praise Your great and holy Name in a joyful and fervent mood, for having delivered our ancestors in Egypt from slavery to freedom and from bondage to liberation.

As we welcome the *Pesach* holiday this evening we voice our deepest concern for the bitter lot of our fellow Jews who are languishing under the yoke of evil decrees and persecution in the Soviet Union, Ethiopia, and in Moslem lands. They are denied the opportunity of observing our festivals and celebrating the feast of unleavened bread, in accordance with our tradition.

May it be Your will, O Rock of Israel and its Redeemer, as You have brought our forefathers out of slavery in Egypt, so may Your mercy encompass our brethren suffering oppression in the Soviet Union, Ethiopia, and in Moslem lands. Redeem them, gather the dispersed families of our people and bring them back to the soil of our ancient land.

May we be worthy to enjoy the *Pesach* holiday together with the whole house of Israel, in freedom and in unity. Amen.

Next Year in Jerusalem!

Distributed by the Commission on Soviet Jewry of the Community Relations Committee, Jewish Federation-Council of Greater Los Angeles.

Resource Sheet 39

SEDER MENU

Gefilte fish with horseradish
Chicken soup with *matzah* balls
Roast turkey with *matzah* stuffing
Vegetable *kugel*
Tossed green salad
Stewed or fresh fruit
Sponge cake, macaroons

This *seder* menu is Ashkenazic. A Sephardic *seder* menu would include many foods which differ from it. A number of Jewish cookbooks include both Ashkenazic and Sephardic menus and recipes.

PASSOVER RECIPES

The following three recipes are reprinted from *The Jewish Holiday Kitchen,* by Joan Nathan. (New York: Schocken Books, Inc., 1979.)

MATZAH STUFFING

What Jewish holiday cookbook would be complete without a good recipe for Passover stuffing?

2 *matzot*
1 large onion
1 large potato
2 eggs
3 tablespoons *matzah* meal
2 stalks celery, finely diced

2 tablespoons chicken fat or *pareve* margarine
1 tablespoon chopped parsley
salt and pepper to taste
paprika to taste

Break the *matzah* in small pieces and soak in hot water. Drain thoroughly; squeeze well. Grate onion and potato and drain off extra water. Combine *matzah,* onion, and potato. Add remaining ingredients.

Makes 4 cups.

VENETIAN CHAROSET

This delicious *charoset* recipe comes from the famous Luzzatto family of Venice. Members of the family have lived in Italy since 1541 and probably before. Names like Benedetto Luzzatto, Simone Luzzatto, Moses Haim Luzzatto, and Samuel David Luzzatto were well known to Italians from the Renaissance to the Enlightenment as authors, professors, and rabbis. Francis Luzzatto of Washington, D.C., works for the Peace Corps and is a keeper of family traditions; the following is his family's recipe.

1½ cups chestnut paste
10 ounces dates, chopped
12 ounces figs, chopped
2 tablespoons poppy seeds
½ cup chopped walnuts
½ cup chopped almonds

½ cup pine nuts
grated rind of 1 orange
½ cup white raisins
¼ cup chopped dried apricots
½ cup brandy
honey to bind

Combine all the ingredients, gradually adding just enough brandy and honey to make the mixture bind.

Makes about 4 cups.

MATZAH BREI
by Jacob Licht

Many consider *matzah brei* a real treat. It is one of those holiday recipes that has nothing whatsoever to do with religion—just gastronomy.

A simple dish, *matzah brei* cannot be made with milk. With milk, it is like pastrami on white bread or chicken livers with mayonnaise. How could Eastern European Jews, with only goose fat available for frying, include milk in *matzah brei?*

Perhaps the fascination with *matzah brei* is the ease of preparation. It consists of soaking *matzah* in water, squeezing very hard, and then frying in grease with or without an egg. It is served with sugar, honey, cinnamon, cinnamon-sugar, and even—by some iconoclasts —with catsup!

3 *matzot*	2 tablespoons fat, *pareve* margarine, or butter for frying
2 large eggs	
salt and freshly ground pepper to taste	cinnamon, cinnamon-sugar, honey, maple syrup, etc.

Break the *matzot* and soak in boiling water for 15 minutes. Drain and squeeze dry. Add the eggs and salt and pepper to taste. Taking tablespoonsful of batter at a time, fry in the chicken fat, margarine, or butter, patting the center down a bit. (You may want larger *matzah* pancakes, in which case just add more batter each time.) When brown on one side, turn and fry on the other. Serve with cinnamon, cinnamon-sugar, honey, maple syrup, or even catsup!

Jacob Licht, father of Rhode Island's former governor Frank Licht, has been a master *matzah brei* maker all his life.

ASHKENAZIC CHAROSET
by the authors

6 large apples, peeled, cored, and coarsely chopped	2 tablespoons honey
	1 teaspoon cinnamon
½ cup chopped walnuts	2 tablespoons sweet red wine

Combine all ingredients and chop together or put in bowl of food processor. Mixture should have the consistency of mortar.

PASSOVER SPONGE CAKE
by Selma Einstein

1 cup Passover *matzah* cake meal	¼ cup Passover potato starch
	1½ cup sugar

1 lemon rind (yellow part)
and some juice

½ cup orange juice and some rind

12 eggs

Separate eggs and beat yolks fluffy. Sift cake meal and potato starch. Add sugar to egg yolks. Add rind and juice. Add cake meal and potato starch. Clean mixer. Beat egg whites until they form peaks. Fold into batter. Pour into ungreased Angel Food spring pan. Bake 1 hour at 325°. Invert pan until cake cools.

For further information on *Pesach,* see *The Jewish Home,* Book 2.

PURIM

GLOSSARY

Purim—

Megillah (pl. *Megillot*)—

Grogger—

Purimspiel—

Shabbat Zachor—

Mishlo'ach Manot—

Hamantashen—

Resource Sheet 41

ON ANTI-SEMITISM

Anti-Semitism is a hatred or hostility directed toward Jews. Although as a technical term it has been used only for the last century, we shall use it to describe all manifestations of hatred of the Jewish people throughout the ages. One of the earliest expressions of an anti-Semitic charge is found in Esther 3:8 when Haman [telling King Ahasuerus] accuses the Jews of being "a certain people, scattered and dispersed among the other peoples in all the provinces of your realm, whose laws are different from those of any other people and who do not obey the king's laws; and it is not in Your Majesty's interest to tolerate them." Note that the verse contains many traditional aspects of anti-Semitism: the homelessness of the Jews, their different social and religious customs, and the belief that they can be dispensed with. (Obeying "the king's laws" refers to religious laws; Jews always obeyed the secular laws of the country they lived in.)

While anti-Jewish hostility existed in Greek and Roman times, pagan anti-Semitism never assumed the tragic proportions of anti-Semitism as practiced in the Christian world. Christianity taught that the Jews were hated by God who rejected them because they refused to accept Jesus and had in fact murdered him. When Christianity became the official religion in European countries, it enacted laws discriminating against Jews. Conversion to Judaism became an offense punishable by death, restrictions against synagogues were decreed, and a movement toward forced conversion of the Jews became strong from the fifth century on. Religious anti-Semitism reached a climax of violence against Jews in the period of the Crusades from 1096 on. Afterwards, Jews were forced to wear special badges. Besides this, Jews were not permitted to own land and had to pay special taxes. During the strife of the Reformation in the sixteenth century the Jews were forced to live in special walled off areas called ghettos. In the nineteenth century, as religious medievalism weakened in Europe, anti-Semitism took on other forms. Thus it was claimed that Jews represented a different race (the Semitic race) and were unable to assimilate into the environment without corrupting society.

Modern anti-Semitism is the result of a long period in which the Christian leaders of Europe treated the Jews as a people apart and as objects of contempt. Once a hostile climate was built up around them and they were made into a hateful minority—not because they did something reprehensible but largely because they had *not* done something, they had not accepted Christianity—it was easy to attack Jews for all kinds of "reasons": they are international bankers, they are communists, they control the press, they wanted to rule the world, etc. People seemed to be ready to believe anything about the Jews. In the past, superstition also played a part. During the Black Death in 1348, when a third to half of the population of some parts of Europe died, people accused the Jews of poisoning the wells in league with the devil and thousands of Jews were tortured and massacred as a result. In the time of Hitler all the old accusations plus some newly invented ones were used as "reasons" for killing Jews. Even today there are extreme anti-Semites; usually they are psychopaths with a strong inferiority complex, who engage in violent acts against Jews for hidden psychological motives. But there are also many "normal" people who have anti-Semitic prejudices which they are "convinced" they are "right" in holding.

The development of the phenomenon we call "anti-Semitism" stems from the attempt of the church during the Middle Ages to force the Jewish people to abandon their religion and join the church. Jews were often forced to listen to sermons in their synagogues by Christian missionaries. Large numbers of Jews died rather than convert. In Spain almost a quarter of a million Jews were forced into exile because they refused to enter the church. Those who decided to convert, however, found that within a few years prejudice was again directed against them. They were suspected of practicing Jewish rituals in the privacy of their homes while outwardly attending the church as good Christians. Such people were called Marranos and for two centuries after the Spanish expulsion in 1492 the Inquisition tortured the Marranos to find out if they were secret Jews.

The United States never had an established church. It was founded by minority religious groups seeking freedom from religious persecution; perhaps we would not have had anti-Semitism in the United States because of its different history, but the people who settled in America were Europeans and they brought the disease with them. While our country has not experienced the violent form of the illness, we have had it in other forms. During the twenties many leading schools (including Harvard) had a quota on the number of

Jewish students they would admit. Very few Jews were permitted to reach executive positions in the fields of banking and insurance, automobiles, aviation, railroads, gas and electric, utilities, in spite of the fact that Jews make up almost 10 percent of the college-trained population in our society.

In the light of these facts it is easy to understand why many Jews have preferred to associate with other Jews. This is especially true of the older generation that lived through the Hitler period.

Introduction to Judaism: Student Manual. Union of American Hebrew Congregations, Pacific Southwest Council. Los Angeles, 1968.

Resource Sheet 42

SONGSHEET

IN SHU-SHU-SHUSHAN

Oh, Haman was a high and mighty bluff
In Shu-Shu-Shushan long ago.
He ordered Mordecai to take his derby off
In Shu-Shu-Shushan long ago.

Chorus

So we sing, so we sing,
So we sing, and raise a row
For Haman he was swinging
While Mordecai was singing
In Shu-Shu-Shushan long ago.

But Mordecai sat and laughed in his face
In Shu-Shu-Shushan long ago.
So Haman swore he'd exterminate his race
In Shu-Shu-Shushan long ago.

(Chorus)

Oh, Esther was a timid, little maid
In Shu-Shu-Shushan long ago.
But Mordecai told her she needn't be afraid
In Shu-Shu-Shushan long ago.

(Chorus)

Ahasuerus was the jolly, little king
In Shu-Shu-Shushan long ago
Who ruined Haman's plot in the merry month of spring
In Shu-Shu-Shushan long ago.

(Chorus)

A WICKED, WICKED MAN

Oh, once there was a wicked, wicked man
And Haman was his name, sir.
He lied and lied about the Jews
Though they were not to blame, sir.

Chorus
Oh, today we'll merry, merry be (3x)
And nosh some hamantashen.

And Esther was the lovely queen
Of King Ahasuerus.
When Haman said he'd kill us all,
Oh my! how he did scare us!

(Chorus)

But Mordecai her cousin bold
Said, "What a dreadful villain;
If we don't act at once, my dear,
Our life's not worth a shillin'."

(Chorus)

When Esther speaking to the king
Of Haman's plot made mention,
"Aha!" said he, "Oh, no he won't;
I'll spoil his bad intention."

(Chorus)

And so, my friend, came to an end
This clever Mr. Smarty,
For he became a wiser man
At Esther's *Purim* party.

(Chorus)

Resource Sheet 43

HAMANTASHEN RECIPE

by Robin Einstein

DOUGH

4 cups sifted all-purpose flour
4 teaspoons baking powder
1 teaspoon salt
1 cup butter or margarine
1 cup granulated sugar

1 cup brown sugar
2 eggs
4 tablespoons milk
2 teaspoons vanilla extract

Mix flour, baking powder, and salt. Cream butter and sugar together. Add eggs. Add the dry ingredients alternately with the milk. Add vanilla. Roll out dough (approximately ¼″ thick) and cut into rounds. (A drinking glass is good to use as a cutter.) Fill the cookies; pinch up sides to form a triangle. Bake in a 375° oven until brown, about 10–15 minutes.

Makes about 80.

FILLING

Many Jewish cookbooks offer different kinds of fillings, such as prune, poppy seed, and nut. However, it is also possible to use ready-made pastry and cake fillings, which come in a variety of flavors and are available in most supermarkets.

Note: This is a basic sugar cookie dough recipe. You may want to use this recipe for holiday cookies. The dough can easily be cut into appropriate shapes, e.g., *dreidels,* stars, and *menorahs* for *Chanukah.*

For further information on *Purim,* see *The Jewish Home,* Book 3.

ROSH HASHANAH

Resource Sheet 44

GLOSSARY

Rosh Hashanah—

High Holy Days—

Shofar—

Chet—

Teshuvah—

Selichot—

Tashlich—

Leshanah Tovah Tikatevu—

Yom Tov—

Gemar Chatimah Tovah—

Machzor—

Resource Sheet 45

ROSH HASHANAH EVE BLESSINGS

CANDLE BLESSING

The observance of *Rosh Hashanah* reminds us that all we say and do stands under judgment: our own and God's. It calls us to turn from old errors and failures and to look ahead with fresh hope and determination.

Let us praise God with this symbol of joy and give thanks for the goodness we have experienced during the past year. May our worship on this day fill us with eagerness to embrace life and to hallow it. May the new year bring renewed strength to our people Israel and peace to the world.

בָּרוּךְ אַתָּה, יְיָ אֱלֹהֵינוּ, מֶלֶךְ הָעוֹלָם, אֲשֶׁר קִדְּשָׁנוּ בְּמִצְוֹתָיו וְצִוָּנוּ לְהַדְלִיק נֵר שֶׁל (שַׁבָּת וְשֶׁל) יוֹם טוֹב.

Baruch Atah Adonai Elohenu Melech ha'olam asher kideshanu be-mitsvotav vetsivanu lehadlik ner shel (Shabbat veshel) Yom Tov.
Blessed is the Lord our God, Ruler of the universe, by whose *mitzvot* we are hallowed, who commands us to kindle the lights of (*Shabbat* and) *Yom Tov.*

KIDDUSH

With the setting of this evening's sun, united with Jews of every place and time, we proclaim a new year of hope. Lord of the universe, let Your light and Your truth come forth to lead us. These flames we kindle are a symbol of Your eternal flame: may they open our eyes to the good we must do, moving us to work for harmony and peace, and so making the world bright with Your presence.

בָּרוּךְ אַתָּה, יְיָ אֱלֹהֵינוּ, מֶלֶךְ הָעוֹלָם, בּוֹרֵא פְּרִי הַגָּפֶן.

Baruch Atah Adonai Elohenu Melech ha'olam Borei peri hagafen.
Blessed is the Lord our God, Ruler of the universe, Creator of the fruit of the vine.

בָּרוּךְ אַתָּה, יְיָ אֱלֹהֵינוּ, מֶלֶךְ הָעוֹלָם, שֶׁהֶחֱיָנוּ וְקִיְּמָנוּ וְהִגִּיעָנוּ לַזְּמַן הַזֶּה.

Baruch Atah Adonai Elohenu Melech ha'olam shehecheyanu vekiyemanu vehigianu lazeman hazeh.
Blessed is the Lord our God, Ruler of the universe, for giving us life, for sustaining us, and for enabling us to reach this season.

HAMOTZI

בָּרוּךְ אַתָּה, יְיָ אֱלֹהֵינוּ, מֶלֶךְ הָעוֹלָם, הַמּוֹצִיא לֶחֶם מִן הָאָרֶץ.

Baruch Atah Adonai Elohenu Melech ha'olam hamotzi lechem min ha'aretz.
Blessed is the Lord our God, Ruler of the universe, who causes bread to come forth from the earth.

APPLES AND HONEY

בָּרוּךְ אַתָּה, יְיָ אֱלֹהֵינוּ, מֶלֶךְ הָעוֹלָם, בּוֹרֵא פְּרִי הָעֵץ.

Baruch Atah Adonai Elohenu Melech ha'olam Borei peri ha'etz.
Blessed is the Lord our God, Ruler of the universe, Creator of the fruit of the tree.

יְהִי רָצוֹן מִלְּפָנֶיךָ, יְיָ אֱלֹהֵינוּ וֵאלֹהֵי אֲבוֹתֵינוּ, שֶׁתְּחַדֵּשׁ עָלֵינוּ שָׁנָה טוֹבָה וּמְתוּקָה.

Yehi ratson milefanecha Adonai Elohenu velohei avotenu shetechadesh alenu shanah tovah umetukah.
Lord our God and God of our people, may the new year be good for us, and sweet.

Stern, Chaim, ed. *Gates of the House.* New York: Central Conference of American Rabbis, 1976.

SCHEMA OF ROSH HASHANAH

EVENING

1. Candle blessing
2. *Kiddush*
3. *Hamotzi*
4. Apples and honey
5. Dinner
6. *Birkat Hamazon* (grace after meals)
7. Services

MORNING

1. Services
2. At home—*Borei peri hagafen, motzi*
3. Lunch
4. *Birkat Hamazon*
5. *Tashlich*

Resource Sheet 47

THE ANNOUNCING TOOL:
A READ-ALOUD MIDRASH FOR
CHILDREN

by Rabbi Marc A. Gellman
Congregation Beth Am, Teaneck, N.J.

A long time ago when all people lived in one place, getting the news was easy. They had yellers who would walk around town and, after no more than a morning of yelling, everyone knew that something special had happened. But, when people began living all over the place, even the yellers couldn't get the news across. Mostly, people just didn't get the news, but some special events just had to be announced, and the arrival of a new year was the most special event of all. So a man named Enoch asked God what to do to get the news of the new year around the world.

God said to Enoch, "You need a special announcing tool—go find one!" The next day Enoch returned with two rocks. "Listen to my fine announcing tool," he said, and he banged the two rocks together making a loud rock-banging noise. God said to Enoch, "What kind of announcing tool is this to tell of the arrival of the new year? Rocks do not make music, they only make noise. The new year is a time for music and singing, not banging and yelling." God frowned at Enoch who scurried off to find a new announcing tool.

The next day Enoch returned with a gong. "Listen to my fine announcing tool which makes a beautiful sound," he said, and he hit the gong which made a gong-ringing sound. God said to Enoch, "What kind of announcing tool is this to tell of the arrival of the new year? The gong does make a beautiful sound, but it is made of iron, and iron is used to make weapons of war. The new year is a time of peace, not war." God frowned at Enoch who scurried off to find a new announcing tool.

The next day Enoch returned with a harp. "Listen to my fine announcing tool which makes a beautiful sound and is not made of iron!" Then Enoch strummed a tune on the harp. God said to Enoch,

"The harp also will not do as an announcing tool for the new year. The harp does indeed make beautiful sounds and it is not a weapon of war, but the harp is too soft a sound to announce the new year. The new year is a time of loud rejoicing, and a loud announcing tool is needed, a tool that will carry the news of the new year from hilltop to hilltop around the world." God frowned at Enoch who scurried off to find a new announcing tool.

The next day Enoch arrived with a golden trumpet. "Listen to my fine announcing tool which makes a beautiful sound, is not made of iron, and is loud enough to carry the news from hilltop to hilltop." Then Enoch blew a loud note on the golden horn. God said to Enoch, "The golden horn is a good announcing tool, but not good enough for the new year. True, the golden horn makes beautiful sounds, is not made of iron, and is loud enough; but the horn is not a natural instrument. It is made by man and not by Me. It is hollow, but it is not naturally hollow. It is made hollow by human hands. It makes a beautiful sound only after it has been pounded and shaped by human hands. The new year is not a time to glorify human creations. The new year is for all creatures, the animals and people as well. Find something to celebrate the new year which is for all My creatures." God frowned at Enoch who scurried off to find a new announcing tool.

The next day Enoch was a little late in coming, but he finally arrived a little out of breath. "I am embarrassed to present my new announcing tool. It is only a ram's horn—not nearly as beautiful as the golden horn, or as sweet and delicate as the harp—but it does make fine sounds and it is not a weapon of war, and it is loud enough to get the news from hilltop to hilltop. I have done nothing to the horn, it is naturally hollow, and it comes from one of Your creatures. But there is just one thing. All the other instruments were easy to make a sound with, but this ram's horn is impossible to play. I blow and blow, and then a toot comes out, and then nothing, and then maybe another toot. I wish it were easier." God smiled the biggest smile at Enoch and taught him how to blow the ram's horn for the big celebration of the new year which was soon to begin.

Moment Magazine, Volume 4, Number 8, September 1979.

ROSH HASHANAH MENU

DINNER

Round *chalah*
Wine for *Kiddush*
Apples and honey
Gefilte fish
Chicken soup
Cucumber salad
Roast turkey
Noodle *kugel*
Carrots
Honey cake
Taiglach
Coffee, tea

ROSH HASHANAH RECIPES

TOVA'S KUGEL
by Tova Halperin

2 (7 oz. each) pkg. flat egg noodles
¼ lb. butter or margarine, melted
¾ cup sugar
2 eggs, lightly beaten
1 tablespoon cinnamon

¾–1 cup raisins
1 cup orange juice
1 cup applesauce
¾ cup sliced almonds or chopped walnuts
1 cup chopped apples (optional)

Boil noodles until almost cooked; drain and run cold water over them. Add other ingredients and pour into a square or rectangular baking dish which was previously greased. Bake at 350° for ¾–1 hour.

TAIGLACH
by Victoria Kelman

6 eggs
2 teaspoons sugar
3 tablespoons oil
4 cups flour (sifted)

1½ teaspoons baking powder
1½ tablespoons grated lemon or orange peel

Mix together and knead until smooth and elastic. Roll into ropes ⅜" in diameter. Cut into pieces ¾" to 1" long. Heat oven to 350°.

Bring following ingredients to boil in flat metal pan.
1 pound honey
1 cup sugar
2 teaspoons ginger

When bubbling, drop the pieces of dough into pan, one by one. Put pan into oven and don't open door for 20 minutes. Take pan out of oven and stir to separate and turn. Add 1 cup walnuts.

Bake 45 minutes to 1 hour altogether, stirring occasionally. Wet a wooden board with cold water. Pour mixture onto board to cool and separate. Sprinkle with sugar and ginger and let cool.

For further information on *Rosh Hashanah,* see *The Jewish Home,* Book 4.

SHABBAT-PART I

Resource Sheet 49

GLOSSARY

Shabbat (Shabbos)—

Kodesh—

Kavanah—

Mitzvah—

Resource Sheet 50

THE MESSIAH IN JUDAISM

The word "messiah" is derived from the Hebrew word *"mashiach,"* which literally means "anointed one." In the days of the Bible, anointing a person with oil was a way of declaring him king. Thus, messiah means king. What is referred to by the term is a flesh-and-blood king, *not* a divine being.

Messianic expectations developed over time. In the fully developed form of this idea, it was believed that the Messiah would (1) establish himself as the king, (2) gain independence for the Jewish people in our own land, (3) be an ideal king, and, (4) with God's help, establish peace, justice, and brotherhood—not only for the Jews, but for all the world.

Throughout our history, there were a number of individuals who claimed to be the Messiah. While each of these people gained some following at first, since *none* of them—*including Jesus*—fulfilled the messianic expectations, no one has been accepted as the Messiah.

The early church realized that Jesus did not do all that was expected of the Messiah. They insisted that he would return to earth some day to complete the task. This doctrine is known as the "Second Coming of Christ." The Jewish view of this is simply "seeing is believing."

Incidentally, knowledgeable Jews don't refer to Jesus as "Christ" since "Christ" is a title meaning "anointed one" and we do not believe that Jesus was the Anointed One. Though Jesus has no role whatsoever in Judaism, most Jews would say that he was a fine teacher whose teachings have had a considerable influence on the world. A good deal of what he taught was basic Judaism.

The person of the Messiah was never really important. What was important was the result of his arrival—the Messianic Age. Reform and Conservative Judaism generally emphasize the need for all people to work for a Messianic Age; Orthodox Jews do maintain the hope for a personal Messiah.

A SAMPLE OF WORLD-TO-COME

When God was about to give the Torah to Israel, He summoned the people and said to them: "My children, I have something precious that I would like to give you for all time, if you will accept My Torah and observe My commandments."

The people then asked: "Master of the universe, what is that precious gift You have for us?"

The Holy One, blessed be He, replied, "It is the world-to-come [the Messianic Age]!"

The people of Israel answered: "Show us a sample of the world-to-come."

The Holy One, blessed be He, said: "The *Shabbat* is a sample of the world-to-come, for that world will be one long *Shabbat.*"

The Midrash.

Resource Sheet 52

THE SABBATH TASTE

There is a legend about Joshua ben Hananiah and the emperor. Rabbi Joshua was very wise and he was often invited to the palace to talk with the emperor.

One day, the emperor happened to be walking through the streets of the Jewish Quarter. He was dressed in the clothes of the common people. He passed through the street of the cobblers and the street of the goldsmiths, the street of the charcoal burners and the street of the weavers. It was Sabbath. The shops were closed. The houses were scrubbed and shining. Their doors were open and the emperor could see inside. The Jews were having their Sabbath meal.

"It must be a wonderful kind of food they are eating," thought the emperor. "They enjoy it so much. You couldn't enjoy a common meal as much as that."

So next day he sent for Rabbi Joshua.

"Rabbi," he said, "will you tell me how the Jews prepare their Sabbath food? I want my cooks to prepare a meal for me just like theirs."

"I will tell you gladly," said Rabbi Joshua.

So the emperor sent word to the royal kitchen and up came all the cooks, the head cook, the first helper to the cook, the second helper to the cook, the pudding maker, and the baker.

They bowed to the emperor. Then they turned to Rabbi Joshua and listened carefully. And Rabbi Joshua told them exactly how the Jews prepared their Sabbath food.

"O Emperor," said the head cook when Joshua had finished, "tomorrow you shall have a meal exactly like the Sabbath meal of the Jews."

"Exactly!" said the first helper to the cook, the second helper, the pudding maker, and the baker. Then they bowed again and went back to the royal kitchen.

Next day the emperor could hardly wait for dinner to begin. A servant appeared. He set a platter of fish before the emperor. The emperor tasted it. He looked puzzled. It didn't have a special taste at all. It was just fish.

A second servant came in. He set a golden bowl of soup before the king. The bowl was golden and the soup was golden. There were noodles in it, fine as thread. The emperor tried a spoonful. "Take it away," he ordered. "It's the kind of soup I get every day."

The head cook came in. He carried a huge platter on his head. There was roast chicken on the platter with a pudding on one side and carrot stew with dumplings on the other. The emperor's mouth watered.

"Now surely," he said, "I shall taste the wonderful taste." He picked up a chicken leg and put it to his mouth. Then he pushed back his plate and left the table.

"Send for Rabbi Joshua," he cried to his servants. "Send for the royal cooks."

The cooks filed into the throne room. Rabbi Joshua followed them.

"Cooks," asked the emperor, "did you prepare the food exactly as Rabbi Joshua told you to?"

"Exactly!" said the head cook.

"Exactly!" said the first helper to the cook, the second helper, the pudding maker, and the baker.

"But Sabbath food *must* have a special taste," the emperor insisted. "I saw the Jews when they ate it. They sang with every bite. You couldn't enjoy everyday food like that."

"O emperor," said Rabbi Joshua, and he smiled. "The Sabbath food *has* a special taste. The taste comes from a certain spice that is in it, a spice called Sabbath."

"Why didn't you say so before? Give me that spice," cried the emperor.

"O emperor," said Rabbi Joshua again, "the spice cannot be given. It comes of itself—to those who love the Sabbath."

The Midrash.

SHABBAT-PART II

Resource Sheet 53

GLOSSARY

Minyan—

Chalah—

Kiddush—

Tsedakah Box—

Havdalah—

Resource Sheet 54

STRUCTURE OF JEWISH WORSHIP: THE SABBATH EVE SERVICE

The page references are for *Gates of Prayer* and refer to the first *Shabbat* evening service. *Gates of Prayer* offers a number of other options.

1. *Candle Lighting* (The lighting of the Sabbath candles should take place at home; it can also take place at the beginning of the evening service.) (P. 117)
2. *Kabbalat Shabbat* (Preliminary psalms, songs, and readings to welcome *Shabbat.*) (Pp. 118–127)
3. *Reader's Kaddish* (P. 128)
4. *Barechu* (The call to worship.) (P. 129)
5. *Blessings before the Shema* (On Creation and Revelation.) (Pp. 129–130)
6. *Shema* (The declaration of a Jew's faith. The *Ve'ahavta*—"You shall love . . ."—is part of the *Shema.* These passages come from Deuteronomy 6:4–9 and Numbers 15:40–41.) (Pp. 130–131)
7. *Redemption* (Includes the *Mi Chamochah?*—"Who is like You?" —from Exodus 15:11, 18.) (Pp. 131–132)
8. *Hashkivenu* (The evening prayer.) (P. 133)
9. *Veshameru* (The people of Israel shall keep the Sabbath. From Exodus 31:16–17) (P. 133)
10. *Tefilah* (Also called *Amidah* or *Shemoneh Esreh.* A series of short blessings, the *Tefilah* is the core of the service. During or after the *Tefilah,* time is given for personal silent prayer or meditation.) (Pp. 134–141)
11. *Kiddush* (*Kiddush* should take place in the home. In addition, it may be placed after the candle lighting, before the Torah service or the sermon, or as the beginning of the *Oneg Shabbat.*) (P. 719)
12. *Torah Service* (The Torah is read at the *Shabbat* morning service. In many Reform congregations, it is read at the *Shabbat* evening service as well.) (Pp. 417–424)
13. *Devar Torah* (Sermon, talk, story, discussion, program, etc.)
14. *Alenu* (The Adoration.) (Pp. 615–616)

15. *A Meditation before Kaddish*
16. *Kaddish* (A praise of God, often recited in memory of those who have died.) (Pp. 628–629)
17. *Closing Song*
18. *Benediction*

Resource Sheet 55

CHART OF POSSIBILITIES AND BEGINNINGS

POSSIBILITIES TO DO

Friday Evening:
Light candles
Kiddush over wine
Chalah
Bless children
Family dinner
Attend services
Make love with spouse

Saturday:
Attend services
Study
Visit friends
Go for a walk
Take a nap
Spend time with each family member
Make *Havdalah*

POSSIBILITIES NOT TO DO

Work at your job
Drive your car
Deal with money
Write
Clean your house
Shop

Two things I will try to do (or not to do):
1._____
2._____

Journal entry: After *Shabbat,* in your Journal, write your feelings about the two things you did or did not do.

Resource Sheet 56

SHABBAT MENUS

FRIDAY NIGHT SHABBAT DINNER

Chalah
Wine for *Kiddush*

I

Gefilte fish
Pickles or cucumber salad
Brisket of beef
Potato *kugel*
Vegetable
Cake, tea, coffee

II

Chicken Soup
Roast chicken or turkey
Noodle *kugel*
Vegetable
Cake, tea, coffee

SHABBAT RECIPES

CHICKEN SOUP
by Selma Einstein

2 3-pound chickens
½ bunch celery
1 bunch carrots
1 onion
2 turnips

2 parsnips
1 rutabaga
½ bunch parsley
1 bay leaf
water

Clean the chickens. Trim extra fat and post-nose. Clean the vegetables. Place chickens and giblets in pot. Add celery, carrots, onion, salt, pepper, turnips, parsnips, rutabaga, parsley, and bay leaf.

Cover chicken and vegetables with water. Cover pot and bring to a boil. Skim off fat. Reduce heat and simmer at least 2 hours.

The chickens can be browned and served or eaten boiled.

To brown, place chickens in roasting pan, put on *pareve* margarine, salt, pepper, paprika, and other seasonings to taste. Bake 30 minutes at 350°.

BRISKET
by Mildred Kessler

1 2-pound first-cut brisket
1 package dry onion soup
paprika

browning and seasoning sauce,
  such as Kitchen Bouquet.
1 glass water

In a hot frying pan, sear meat to seal in juices. Put meat in roaster. Add 1 package of dry onion soup and 1 glass water in roaster. Sprinkle meat with paprika and add some browning and seasoning sauce. Cover roaster, keeping a high flame until water boils. When the water boils, put on low flame and cook one hour on each side.

POTATO KUGEL

4 eggs
8 medium Idaho potatoes
1 large onion, peeled and cut in
  pieces
6 tablespoons *matzah* meal

1½ teaspoons baking powder
2 teaspoons salt
¼ teaspoon pepper
¼ cup melted chicken fat or
  pareve margarine

Preheat oven to 375°. Break the eggs in a medium bowl and set aside. Grate the potatoes and onion in a food processor or by hand. Pour into a large strainer. Drain water and combine potatoes and onions with the eggs. Stir thoroughly and add the *matzah* meal, baking powder, salt, pepper, and chicken fat or margarine. Turn into a large greased souffle dish. Bake in the oven 30–45 minutes, until golden brown.
  Serves 8–10.

MATZAH BALLS
(KNEIDLACH)

4 eggs, slightly beaten
4 tablespoons chicken fat
1 cup *matzah* meal
2 teaspoons salt

4 tablespoons chicken soup or water
4 quarts salted water

In a medium bowl, beat the eggs and the fat together. Stir in the *matzah* meal and salt. Add the chicken soup or water. Refrigerate for 1 hour or more to permit the meal to absorb the liquids.

In a 6-quart pot with a lid, bring the salted water to a boil. Reduce the water to a simmer and drop in balls of the *matzah* mixture about 1½" in diameter. Cover the pot and simmer for 20 minutes. When they are ready, they may be placed in chicken soup to serve.

Makes 20.

Note: There is a light-and-fluffy school of *matzah* balls and a cannon-ball school. These belong to the former and achieved by a simple trick. *Never* take the lid off the pot while they are cooking, or you will boil instead of steam the dumplings.

If you have extras, they can be served the next day. Although they will be a little denser in texture, they will still be tasty. They are also very good as a starch when browned in margarine. They must be refrigerated thoroughly before frying or they will fall apart.

Nathan, Joan. *The Jewish Holiday Kitchen.* New York: Schocken Books, Inc., 1979. (*Potato kugel* and *matzah ball* recipes appear in the book.)

For further information on *Shabbat,* see *The Jewish Home,* Book 1.

SHAVUOT

Resource Sheet 57

GLOSSARY

Shavuot—

Confirmation—

Blintzes—

Resource Sheet 58

TANACH, THE BIBLE

by Rabbi Lawrence Jackofsky

The Bible is composed of thirty-nine books divided into three major sections. The first letter of the Hebrew name of the first section— *T*orah (Law)—is combined with the first letters of the two other sections—*N*evi'im (Prophets) and *K*etuvim (Writings)—to create the traditional Hebrew name—*TaNaCH*—for the total Bible.

I. TORAH

(Also called *Chumash,* the Hebrew word for "five"; the Five Books of Moses; or Pentateuch, the Greek word for five books.)

Traditionally, Torah is read on three mornings of the week: Monday, Thursday, and Saturday. Each week the portion follows a progressive pattern so that in one year (according to an ancient Palestinian custom, in three years) the entire Torah scroll is read. Each week's reading is called a *"sidrah"* (from the Hebrew word *seder,* "order") and is set in an order by the Hebrew calendar.

Its contents:
A. Genesis (*Bereshit,* "In the beginning").

Bereshit tells the story from the creation of the world to the death of Joseph in Egypt. The first eleven chapters deal with universal history, and the remainder with the lives of Abraham, Isaac, Jacob, and their families. According to tradition, the total elapsed time adds up to 1946 (or 1948) years. The overriding thrust is the establishment of God's role in human affairs and of man's interaction with God, other human beings, and the self.

B. Exodus (*Shemot,* "Names").

Shemot is a natural continuation of *Bereshit* where the lives of the Patriarchs of the Hebrew people are described; *Shemot* tells the beginning of the people itself. It records Israel's enslavement in Egypt and the deliverance from the house of bondage. It describes the institution of the Passover, the covenant at Mount Sinai, and the organization of public worship that was to make Israel into "a kingdom of priests and a holy nation." It recounts the murmurings and backslidings of Israel, as well as the divine guidance and instruction vouchsafed to it; the apostasy of the golden calf, as well as the supreme Revelation that followed it—the Revelation of the Divine Being as "God."

"Nearly all the foundations on which Jewish life is built—the Ten Commandments, the historic festivals, the leading principles of civil law—are contained in the Book of Exodus." (Dr. J. H. Hertz)

C. Leviticus (*Vayikra*, "And He called . . .").

Vayikra contains only a few bits of narrative. It is essentially a compendium of law as enumerated by Bernard J. Bamberger in *The Torah: A Modern Commentary* (UAHC):

Laws of sacrifice: Chapters 1–7.

The dedication of the Tabernacle and the ordination of the priests, with certain attendant events: Chapters 8 through 10.

Dietary laws: Chapter 11, verses 1 through 23.

Laws of defilement and purification: Chapter 11, verses 24 through 25, verse 33.

The Day of Atonement: Chapter 16.

Additional laws about sacrifice and food: Chapter 17.

Permitted and forbidden sex relations: Chapters 18 and 20.

The Law of Holiness—ethical and ritual: Chapter 19.

Laws for the priesthood: Chapters 21 and 22.

The Sabbath and festival calendar: Chapter 23.

Two laws and an incident involving blasphemy: Chapter 24.

The sabbatical and jubilee years: Chapter 25.

An exhortation, containing blessings for the observance of the law and curses for its violation: Chapter 26.

Laws concerning vows, gifts, and dues: Chapter 27.

D. Numbers (*Bemidbar,* from the fifth word in the opening chapter, *bemidbar,* "in the wilderness").

Numbers was chosen from the Greek ("Arithmoi") and the Roman ("Numeri") sources for the name of the book in recognition of the extensive statistical material which is found in the opening chapters.

There is a desert motif that underlies *Bemidbar.* This book continues where *Shemot* left off, as God's special people Israel is subjected to special laws and obligations which are designed to safeguard its holiness. As the narrative unfolds, we are told how Israel continues to fall short of its goals and how God, time and again, was disappointed with God's people. Though individuals were punished and a whole generation was condemned to die in the wilderness, the covenant was not abrogated. The sanctuary, with its divine manifestation, remained in the midst of the camp, and God never ceased to guide and protect. (To many this period of wandering is seen as a trial of faith.) At the end of *Bemidbar* there emerges the vision of a new nation which will go on to possess the Holy Land as a Holy People.

E. Deuteronomy (*Devarim,* "Words").

The oldest name of this book was *"Mishneh Torah,"* repetition of the Torah, found in Chapter 17:18.

Devarim, although it has an affinity with the four previous books in the historical, legal, and narrative senses, is unique in that it contains a great deal of oratory. The Lawgiver (God) has brought Israel to the borders of the Holy Land. He, through Moses, recounts in three discourses the events of the forty years of wanderings, and He warns against the temptations awaiting them in Canaan. He promises divine judgment for disobedience as well as divine blessing for faithful observance of the *mitzvot* (commandments). As *Devarim* concludes, Moses addresses his people for the last time before his death and blesses them. Joshua is appointed leader over the people and is ordained by Moses. Moses is buried, "and no one knows his burial place to this day." (34:6)

"Never again did there arise in Israel a prophet like Moses—whom the Lord singled out, face to face." (34:10)

II. NEVI'IM (PROPHETS)

Immediately after reading the *sidrah,* a selection from *Nevi'im* is read. There is always some similarity or connection between that which is read from *Torah* and that which is read from *Nevi'im.* This reading is referred to as *"haftarah"* ("conclusion").

Its contents:
There are twenty-one books arranged in two parts:

A. The Former Prophets (Nonliterary Prophets).

The prophets that we encounter are found in the narrative of the story of the settlement of the people into Canaan, the development of the kingdoms of Judah and Israel, and the founding of a socioreligious community.

Many of the biblical characters are considered to have the status of "prophet," judge, or leader (Joshua, Samuel, Elisha, Deborah, David, Elijah, etc.).

Simply stated the characters we encounter are at the earlier stage of the history of the period of national life and they themselves do not set down bodies of writings in this section, hence, the terms "former" and "nonliterary."

The Former Prophets consist of six books:

1. Joshua
2. Judges
3. I Samuel
4. II Samuel
5. I Kings
6. II Kings

B. The Latter Prophets (Literary Prophets).

Each of the fifteen has a message for the people Israel who now (eighth century B.C.E. to fifth century B.C.E.) have strayed from the moral path *(collectively)*. Each is considered God's messenger; each has been chosen to speak out about the ills of society. They do not foretell the future in the strict sense of the word, only what could happen if the people do or do not repent.

The Latter Prophets are divided into: the Major Prophets (those whose books are lengthy):

1. Isaiah
2. Jeremiah
3. Ezekiel

and the Minor Prophets (those whose books are relatively short):

1. Hosea
2. Joel
3. Amos
4. Obadiah
5. Jonah*
6. Micah
7. Nahum
8. Habakkuk
9. Zephaniah
10. Haggai
11. Zechariah
12. Malachi

Note: Many problems with his status according to the Rabbis.

III. KETUVIM (WRITINGS)

This section, totaling thirteen books, is the third and last section of the *TaNaCH*. It is a mixed anthology of literary pieces and stories relevant to our people. Although in existence before, these writings were officially admitted to the Bible (canonized) by 90 C.E.

Its contents:

A. Poetic Books.
   1. Psalms—express the doubts, hopes, the faith and desire, prayers of their authors.
   2. Proverbs—cogent sayings pertaining to living.
   3. Job—story of how Satan, with God's consent, tested Job to learn if Job was really as righteous as he appeared.

B. The Five Scrolls.
   Each is read in the synagogue in scroll form on one of the Jewish holidays.
   1. Book of Esther—*Purim.*
   2. Ecclesiastes (deals with the purpose and the often-futile nature of life)—*Sukot.*
   3. Song of Songs—*Pesach.*
   4. Story of Ruth—*Shavuot.*
   5. Book of Lamentations—*Tishah Be'av,* 9th of month of Av (July or August of the secular calendar).

C. Prophetic Book—Daniel (stirring faith in God).

D. Historical Books.
   1. Ezra
   2. Nehemiah
   3. I Chronicles
   4. II Chronicles

Note: According to Jewish tradition, the Bible contains only twenty-four books: I Samuel and II Samuel are counted as one book; I Kings and II Kings are counted as one book; the 12 Minor Prophets are counted together as one book; the Book of Ezra and the Book of Nehemiah comprise one book; and I Chronicles and II Chronicles comprise one book.

Resource Sheet 59

SHAVUOT EVE BLESSINGS

CANDLE BLESSING

בָּרוּךְ אַתָּה, יְיָ אֱלֹהֵינוּ, מֶלֶךְ הָעוֹלָם, אֲשֶׁר קִדְּשָׁנוּ בְּמִצְוֹתָיו,
וְצִוָּנוּ לְהַדְלִיק נֵר שֶׁל (שַׁבָּת וְשֶׁל) יוֹם טוֹב.

Baruch Atah Adonai Elohenu Melech ha'olam asher kideshanu be-mitsvotav vetsivanu lehadlik ner shel (Shabbat veshel) Yom Tov.
Blessed is the Lord our God, Ruler of the universe, by whose *mitzvot* we are hallowed, who commands us to kindle the lights of (*Shabbat* and) *Yom Tov*.

KIDDUSH

Shavuot teaches us that only by living under laws of truth and justice do we find happiness and hallow our lives.

With wine, our symbol of joy, we celebrate this day and its holiness, and we give thanks for the revelation of Torah and the first fruits of earth's goodness. May our worship help us to live in the light of Torah, and may we give of the first fruits of our strength for the well-being of our community and our people.

בָּרוּךְ אַתָּה, יְיָ אֱלֹהֵינוּ, מֶלֶךְ הָעוֹלָם, בּוֹרֵא פְּרִי הַגָּפֶן.

Baruch Atah Adonai Elohenu Melech ha'olam Borei peri hagafen.
Blessed is the Lord our God, Ruler of the universe, Creator of the fruit of the vine.

בָּרוּךְ אַתָּה, יְיָ אֱלֹהֵינוּ, מֶלֶךְ הָעוֹלָם, שֶׁהֶחֱיָנוּ וְקִיְּמָנוּ וְהִגִּיעָנוּ
לַזְּמַן הַזֶּה.

Baruch Atah Adonai Elohenu Melech ha'olam shehecheyanu vekiyemanu vehigianu lazeman hazeh.
Blessed is the Lord our God, Ruler of the universe, for giving us life, for sustaining us, and for enabling us to reach this season.

HAMOTZI

בָּרוּךְ אַתָּה, יְיָ אֱלֹהֵינוּ, מֶלֶךְ הָעוֹלָם, הַמּוֹצִיא לֶחֶם מִן
הָאָרֶץ.

*Baruch Atah Adonai Elohenu Melech ha'olam hamotzi lechem min
ha'aretz.*

Blessed is the Lord our God, Ruler of the universe, who causes bread
to come forth from the earth.

Stern, Chaim, ed. *Gates of the House*. New York: Central Conference of
American Rabbis, 1976.

Resource Sheet 60

TERMS RELATED TO MAJOR WORKS OF JEWISH LITERATURE

TaNaCH

Bible

Mishnah

Gemara

Talmud

Midrash

Resource Sheet 61

DAIRY MENU

Borscht
Blintzes and sour cream
Assorted cheeses
Assorted breads (*chalah,* pumpernickel, rye)
Herring or smoked fish
Tuna fish salad
Vegetable plate (scallions, cucumbers, radishes, tomatoes)
Fruit
Cake

A typical dairy meal includes a selection of these foods. It is not necessary to have all of these foods at any given meal.

DAIRY RECIPES

BLINTZES
by Mildred Kessler

Filling

1-pound pot style cheese	1 egg, beaten
(or ½-pound cottage cheese	½ teaspoon salt
plus ½-pound hoop cheese or	3 tablespoons sugar
farmer cheese)	1 tablespoon sour cream

Mix all ingredients together in large bowl.

Shell

4 eggs, beaten	⅝ cup water
1 cup flour	salt

Mix all ingredients together in bowl until smooth. Heat butter in a small frying pan. Pan should be hot before putting batter in, but fry on a medium or medium-high flame. Pour about 2 tablespoons batter into pan; tilt pan until the bottom is evenly coated. Excess may be poured back into bowl. Fry until browned on bottom; then turn out onto a paper towel. Shell should be like a very thin pancake.

Put about 1 tablespoon of filling in the middle of the browned side of the shell; fold up all four sides. Fry on both sides in a frying pan until golden brown. Serve with sour cream or preserves.

Makes about 15.

Note: Many Jewish cookbooks offer a variety of different fillings including fruit fillings.

For further information on *Shavuot,* see *The Jewish Home,* Book 5, and *Keeping Posted,* Vol XXIV, No. 6, March 1979 on "Jewish Law."

SIMCHAT TORAH

GLOSSARY

Simchat Torah—

Torah—

TaNaCH—

Bimah—

Aliyah—

Parashah—

Shemini Atzeret—

Hakafah (pl. *Hakafot*)—

Resource Sheet 63

SONGSHEET

TORAT CHAYIM

Torat chayim, torat chayim utsedakah
Torat chayim, torat chayim uverachah
Rachamim vechayim
Vechayim veshalom
Rachamim vechayim
Vechayim veshalom
Shalom.
(Torah of life and righteousness and blessing and mercy and peace.)

YI-YI-YI-YISRAEL

Yi-yi-yi-Yisrael
Yi-Yisrael
Ve'oraita
Chad hu.
(2x)
Torah ora, torah ora
Halleluyah, halleluyah.
(2x)
(The people of Israel and Torah are one. Torah is light. Hallelujah!)

AL SHELOSHAH DEVARIM

Al sheloshah devarim
Ha'olam omed
Al hatorah,
Ve'al ha'avodah,
Ve'al gemilut chasadim.
(The world depends on three things: on Torah, on worship, and on loving deeds.)

Resource Sheet 64

THE JEWS OF SILENCE

by Elie Wiesel

... Longbeards and workers, old and young, widows and lovely girls, students and bureaucrats. Among them there were many who had never prayed but who had come to watch the processions and to honor the Torah.

Processions? How could they lead a procession through this mob? The Jews formed an impenetrable living mass. No matter. Here everything was possible. It would take time, but no matter. They had the time, and patience too. Somehow the parade would pass. In the meantime they sang, louder and louder. They were all looking at us, the guests, as if to say, "Well, what's with you? Let's hear something from you." The entire Israeli diplomatic corps was present, together with their wives and children. We sang, "Gather our scattered ones from among the nations, and our dispersed from the corners of the world." Five times, ten times. A number of the diplomats belonged to left-wing parties. In their youth they had scorned religion, and religious people in particular. Tonight they celebrated the holiday with chasidic enthusiasm and abandon. Differences of opinion and class were left behind. An American writer once told me, "As I stood among the Jews of Russia, I became a Jew." He was not alone; many who come here as Israelis also return home as Jews.

"Outside they are turning the world upside down."

Should we go out? There was still time. Here, too, the world was in uproar. Men who had not sung for a year were raising their voices in song. Men who had not seen a Torah all year long were embracing and kissing it with a love bequeathed to them from generations past. Old men lifted their grandchildren onto their shoulders, saying, "Look, and remember." The children looked in wonder and laughed, uncertain what was happening. No matter; they would understand later, and they would remember. Tzvikah, the vocalist in the Israeli corps, assembled his chorus and gave them the pitch, "David, king of Israel, lives and endures." There was not a Jew in the hall who was not prepared to give his life defending that assertion.

The dignitaries had made their way back to the pulpit. The first procession was over. The *gabbai* announced that all guests were to take part in the second, and the congregation responded with new bursts of song. From one corner came an Israeli tune, *"Hevenu Shalom Aleichem,"* "We have brought peace unto you"; from another, *"Hava Nagilah,"* "Come let us rejoice." A third group preferred a traditional song, "Blessed is our God who created us in His honor and separated us from the nations and implanted in us eternal life." Instead of resisting one another, the various songs seemed to fuse into a single melodic affirmation. Those who had spent years in prison or in Siberia, those who had only recently become aware of their Jewishness now proclaimed their unity: one people, one Torah. Each of them had stood once at the foot of Mount Sinai and heard the word, *"Anochi"*—I am the Lord your God. Each of them had received the promise of eternity.

We held the scrolls tightly to our chests and tried to make our way through the congregation. But instead of opening a path for us they pressed in closer, as if to block the way completely. They wanted us to stay among them. We were surrounded by a sea of faces, creased, joyful, unmasked. Hats of all kinds, skullcaps of every color, handkerchiefs in place of head covering. A young girl clapped her hands, an old man lifted up his eyes as if in prayer, a laborer sighed joyfully. Old men and their children and their children's children—everyone wanted to touch the Torah, to touch us. Everyone had something to whisper in our ears, a blessing or a secret. I have never in my life received so many blessings, never in my life been surrounded by so much good will and love. One pressed my hand, a second patted my arm, a third held my clothing. They would not let us move forward. They seemed to be trying to stop the progress of time. Through us they became freer, came closer to the reality of their dreams. They looked upon us as redeeming and protective angels. The fact that we were different, unafraid was sufficient to elevate us in their eyes to the stature of saints and wonder workers. When I was young, we used to surround the holy *rebbe* in this fashion, begging him to intercede for us before the heavenly tribunal. But, here, they asked for nothing. On the contrary, they brought us their gifts, their love, their blessings. Hundreds of them. Be healthy! Be strong! Be courageous! May we see you in the years to come! May we all live until that day! May you prosper! And may you sing! Do you hear? Just sing! A few went further, giving vent to their inmost feelings, but always in a whisper: I have a brother in Israel, a sister in Jerusalem, an uncle in Haifa. Short notices: brother, sister, grandfather, uncle, grandson. No names. They simply wanted us to know that a part of them was there, in the land of Israel. Others used clichés that in any other context would have produced smiles of condescension or contempt. "The people of Israel lives"; "the eternity of Israel shall not prove false"; "the redeemer shall come to Zion soon in our days." A Jew with a laborer's cap falling over his brow pushed forward and announced that he had something to tell me but no one was to hear. He began to hum in my ear the words of *"Hatikvah,"* finished the first stanza, and disappeared, his face alight with victory. A woman pleaded with me, "Say something to my daughter. I brought her so she would see Jews who are not ashamed or afraid." The girl was very beautiful, dark, and mysterious, with flashing eyes. She said something in Russian; I answered in Hebrew. Neither of us understood the other; yet somehow we did. Her mother was satisfied; she kissed my hand, murmuring, "Thank you, thank you. Will we ever see you again?" I didn't know what to say. I forgot everything I knew, except those two words: thank you, thank you. Thank you for the gift of this moment, thank you for being alive, for enduring, for knowing how to rejoice and to hope and to dream. Thank you for being Jews like us. And a thousand and one thanks for finding the strength to thank a Jew like me for being a Jew.

They came in droves. From near and far, from downtown and the suburbs, from the university and from the factories, from school dormitories and from the Komsomol club. They came in groups; they came alone. But, once here, they became a single body, voicing a song of praise to the Jewish people and its will to live.

How many were there? Ten thousand? Twenty thousand? More. About thirty thousand. The crush was worse than it had been inside the synagogue. They filled the whole street, spilled over into courtyards, dancing and singing, dancing and singing. They seemed to hover in midair, Chagall-like, floating above the mass of shadows and colors below, above time, climbing a Jacob's ladder that reached to the heavens, if not higher.

Tomorrow they would descend and scatter, disappear into the innermost parts of Moscow, not to be heard from for another year. But they would return and bring more with them. The line will never break; one who has come will always return.

I moved among them like a sleepwalker, stunned by what I saw and heard, half disbelieving my own senses. I had known they would come, but not in such numbers; I had known they would celebrate, but not that their celebration would be so genuine and so deeply Jewish.

They sand and danced, talked among themselves or with strangers. They were borne along on a crest that seemed incapable of breaking. Their faces reflected a special radiance, their eyes the age-old flame that burned in the house of their ancestors—to which they seemed finally to have returned.

I was swept along in the current, passing from one group to another, from one circle to the next, sharing their happiness and absorbing the sound of their voices.

Wiesel, Elie. *The Jews of Silence.* Translated by Neal Kozodoy. New York: Holt, Rinehart and Winston, 1966.

Resource Sheet 65

CARRYING AROUND THE TORAH

by Sherry H. Bissell

I remember vividly the first time I carried the Torah around the sanctuary on *Simchat Torah.* Up until that time, the Torah had always seemed so very heavy—almost cumbersome, too stiff. That night, it can only be a miracle, it changed.

There I was lined up on the *bimah* to carry the Torah. I remember being handed a very large one, feeling its weight, and walking down the steps very carefully.

Then all of a sudden—a child reached over to touch the Torah, and another. I leaned over to them very cautiously (for, if I dropped the Torah, it meant a forty-day fast, and I love food). But then it happened. I looked at their faces and smiled. Suddenly the Torah began to lighten. I walked with a lighter step. As each hand touched the Torah—or as each person touched me, as I saw the laughter in the children's eyes, the longing in the old persons' faces—I was transported. I lightly stepped into a moment, a relationship with every person throughout the generations who had shared this moment. Each person who reached for the Torah that I had clasped to my chest made the Torah become lighter.

All of a sudden I was no longer walking. I was dancing. The Torah was lifted towards the people, the children. I carried it with joy, with love, and with pride. As I was going up the stairs to hand the Torah to the next person, I felt that a part of me was being handed to the next person and that I had experienced true *Simchat Torah,* a joyous moment.

SUKOT

Resource Sheet 66

GLOSSARY

Sukot—

Sukah (pl. *Sukot*)—

Ushpizin—

Lulav—

Etrog—

Hakafah (pl. *Hakafot*)—

FAMILY TREE

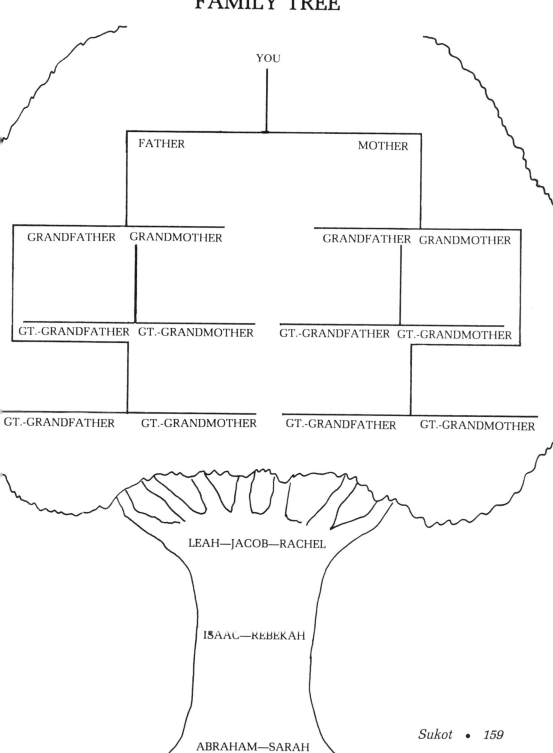

YOU

FATHER

MOTHER

GRANDFATHER GRANDMOTHER

GRANDFATHER GRANDMOTHER

GT.-GRANDFATHER GT.-GRANDMOTHER

GT.-GRANDFATHER GT.-GRANDMOTHER

GT.-GRANDFATHER GT.-GRANDMOTHER

GT.-GRANDFATHER GT.-GRANDMOTHER

LEAH—JACOB—RACHEL

ISAAC—REBEKAH

ABRAHAM—SARAH

Resource Sheet 68

THE MYTHIC PAST

by Linda Thal

When we work up from Abraham and Sarah, the first Jews, we eventually stop being able to name names of the patriarchs and matriarchs and must continue the connection with the Jewish people via socio/historical events and movements, e.g., the Exodus/Sinai experience, the destruction of the Temple, the culture of the *shtetl* (the small Jewish settlements of Eastern Europe), the Holocaust, the rebirth of Israel.

For every Jew, the links between the two points at which we stop being able to name actual names are made up of a series of mythical connections which we claim to have to all these events of Jewish history. One of the ways we make these connections real is by re-enacting the experiences of our assumed ancestors. And, because these connections are real in a mythic way rather than in a documented historical way, it is just as possible for a first generation Jew as a tenth or twentieth generation Jew to make the connections real for him/her self.

Therefore, the holiday of *Sukot,* being the first of several examples of holidays in which we reenact historical experiences of our Jewish ancestors—in this case the forty years the Israelites wandered in the desert after the Exodus from Egypt and prior to their entering the Promised Land—provides us with a first opportunity for making that link.

While *Sukot* is primarily an agricultural celebration, Jewish holidays almost always have a historical dimension too. The booths (*sukot* in Hebrew), which were essentially huts used by farmers during the harvest, were given a transformed meaning as the huts in which the Jews dwelt as they wandered in the desert.

This is probably a fictional transformation, but it doesn't bother us because something can be very real for us at the same time that we are aware that it has a fictional or mythic basis.

Resource Sheet 69

PLANS FOR BUILDING A SUKAH

PLANS

The easiest way to build a *sukah* is with cement blocks, 2 × 4 standards, and improvised walls. Remember that the number of walls required is related to the forms of the Hebrew letters ה כ ס of the word *sukah:* 2½ walls, 3 walls, or 4 walls. All of these are permissible. If you can use the back wall of a house or garage as one of the walls, do so. Stack 3 cement blocks in each corner and insert 7-foot 2 × 4s into the air holes of the blocks. Connect the 2 × 4s with 1 × 2s across the middle and the top. Stretch cloth (or nail ¼-inch plywood, if you can afford it) over the frame and one wall is complete. One wall can serve as the entrance if covered with cloth on a wire track. Place some 1 × 1s running in both directions on the roof and cover that with rushes or pine boughs. The entire roof must be made of organic material. Remember to let the stars shine through!

A sample *sukah* might be a 7-foot cube, for which the following materials would be necessary: 12 cement blocks, 4 pieces of 2″ × 2″ × 7½′, 7 pieces of 1″ × 2″ × 7½′, 8 pieces of 1″ × 1″ × 8′, enough cloth or plywood to cover 3 walls, cloth drape for entrance wall, nails, binding twine, greens for roofing.

You might want the challenge of not using nails, and binding with rope at all joints. It can be done and a fine binding is a beautiful thing to see.

DECORATIONS

Here you can do as you please. Everything's possible from traditional fruit hanging to *ushpizin* posters to printed murals to strung macaroni, gourds, origami, paper chains, etc. Some way should be found not to waste too much fruit in these days of hungry nations.

People with families should perhaps divide the *sukah* into areas, with one person decorating each area. Put in a carpet—that adds a lot of class. An electric light can be installed. Use a garage-style rubber-insulated socket.

Remember never to make the *sukah* overly comfortable. It should shake in the wind. One last thing—once you build it, use it. Eat every meal there (including breakfast). Sleep in it if you can. Invite guests to your *sukah* and share it with all who have none. Always invite the guest of the day according to the *ushpizin* ritual. When you finally break it down, store the material for next year's festival with the understanding and hope that you may not need it again. For, if the Messiah comes before next *Sukot,* we will all sit together under the *Sukah* of *Shalom* and partake of the Great Feast of Leviathan.

Siegel, Richard; Strassfeld, Michael; and Strassfeld, Sharon, compilers and eds. *The First Jewish Catalog.* Philadelphia: The Jewish Publication Society of America, 1973.

Resource Sheet 70

SUKOT EVE/SIMCHAT TORAH EVE BLESSINGS

CANDLE BLESSING

בָּרוּךְ אַתָּה, יְיָ אֱלֹהֵינוּ, מֶלֶךְ הָעוֹלָם, אֲשֶׁר קִדְּשָׁנוּ בְּמִצְוֹתָיו,
וְצִוָּנוּ לְהַדְלִיק נֵר שֶׁל (שַׁבָּת וְשֶׁל) יוֹם טוֹב.

Baruch Atah Adonai Elohenu Melech ha'olam asher kideshanu be-mitsvotav vetsivanu lehadlik ner shel (Shabbat veshel) Yom Tov.
Blessed is the Lord our God, Ruler of the universe, by whose *mitzvot* we are hallowed, who commands us to kindle the lights of (*Shabbat* and) *Yom Tov.*

KIDDUSH FOR SUKOT
Sukot teaches us to give thanks for the harvest of fruit and grain, and to share these and all our blessings with others.

With wine, our symbol of joy, we celebrate this day and its holiness, and give thanks to God, who has been with us in all our wanderings, and who sustains us from year to year by the fruitfulness of the world. Thankful for God's goodness, may we work to bring blessing to all the world.

KIDDUSH FOR ATZERET-SIMCHAT TORAH
This festival teaches us that the study of Torah never ends, and that its influence can fill our lives with the beauty of holiness.

With wine, our symbol of joy, we celebrate this day and its holiness, giving thanks for the great teachers of every generation. May our worship make us eager to study our heritage and to use its knowledge in the service of humanity.

בָּרוּךְ אַתָּה, יְיָ אֱלֹהֵינוּ, מֶלֶךְ הָעוֹלָם, בּוֹרֵא פְּרִי הַגָּפֶן.

Baruch Atah Adonai Elohenu Melech ha'olam Borei peri hagafen.
Blessed is the Lord our God, Ruler of the universe, Creator of the fruit of the vine.

בָּרוּךְ אַתָּה, יְיָ אֱלֹהֵינוּ, מֶלֶךְ הָעוֹלָם, שֶׁהֶחֱיָנוּ וְקִיְּמָנוּ וְהִגִּיעָנוּ לַזְּמַן הַזֶּה.

Baruch Atah Adonai Elohenu Melech ha'olam shehecheyanu vekiyemanu vehigianu lazeman hazeh.

Blessed is the Lord our God, Ruler of the universe, for giving us life, for sustaining us, and for enabling us to reach this season.

HAMOTZI

בָּרוּךְ אַתָּה, יְיָ אֱלֹהֵינוּ, מֶלֶךְ הָעוֹלָם, הַמּוֹצִיא לֶחֶם מִן הָאָרֶץ.

Baruch Atah Adonai Elohenu Melech ha'olam hamotzi lechem min ha'aretz.

Blessed is the Lord our God, Ruler of the universe, who causes bread to come forth from the earth.

BLESSINGS IN THE SUKAH

בָּרוּךְ אַתָּה, יְיָ אֱלֹהֵינוּ, מֶלֶךְ הָעוֹלָם, אֲשֶׁר קִדְּשָׁנוּ בְּמִצְוֹתָיו וְצִוָּנוּ לֵישֵׁב בַּסֻּכָּה.

Baruch Atah Adonai Elohenu Melech ha'olam asher kideshanu be-mitsvotav vetsivanu leshev basukah.

Blessed is the Lord our God, Ruler of the universe, by whose *mitzvot* we are hallowed, who commands us to celebrate in the *sukah.*

בָּרוּךְ אַתָּה, יְיָ אֱלֹהֵינוּ, מֶלֶךְ הָעוֹלָם,
אֲשֶׁר קִדְּשָׁנוּ בְּמִצְוֹתָיו וְצִוָּנוּ עַל־נְטִילַת לוּלָב.

Baruch Atah Adonai Elohenu Melech ha'olam asher kideshanu be-mitsvotav vetsivanu al netilat lulav.

Blessed is the Lord our God, Ruler of the universe, by whose *mitzvot* we are hallowed, who gives us the *mitzvah* of the *lulav.*

USHPIZIN—WELCOMING GUESTS INTO THE SUKAH

1. Abraham, exalted guest, you are welcome here, along with Isaac, Jacob, Joseph, Moses, Aaron, and David.

   Sarah, exalted guest, you are welcome here, along with Rebekah, Rachel, Leah, Miriam, Hannah, and Deborah.

2. Isaac, exalted guest, you are welcome here, along with Abraham, Jacob, Joseph, Moses, Aaron, and David.

Rebekah, exalted guest, you are welcome here, along with Sarah, Rachel, Leah, Miriam, Hannah, and Deborah.

3. Jacob, exalted guest, you are welcome here, along with Abraham, Isaac, Joseph, Moses, Aaron, and David.

Rachel, exalted guest, you are welcome here, along with Sarah, Rebekah, Leah, Miriam, Hannah, and Deborah.

4. Joseph, exalted guest, you are welcome here, along with Abraham, Isaac, Jacob, Moses, Aaron, and David.

Leah, exalted guest, you are welcome here, along with Sarah, Rebekah, Rachel, Miriam, Hannah, and Deborah.

5. Moses, exalted guest, you are welcome here, along with Abraham, Isaac, Jacob, Joseph, Aaron, and David.

Miriam, exalted guest, you are welcome here, along with Sarah, Rebekah, Rachel, Leah, Hannah, and Deborah.

6. Aaron, exalted guest, you are welcome here, along with Abraham, Isaac, Jacob, Joseph, Moses, and David.

Hannah, exalted guest, you are welcome here, along with Sarah, Rebekah, Rachel, Leah, Miriam, and Deborah.

7. David, exalted guest, you are welcome here, along with Abraham, Isaac, Jacob, Joseph, Moses, and Aaron.

Deborah, exalted guest, you are welcome here, along with Sarah, Rebekah, Rachel, Leah, Miriam, and Hannah.

Stern, Chaim, ed. *Gates of the House.* New York: Central Conference of American Rabbis, 1976.

MIDRASH LEVITICUS RABBAH 30:12

Another exposition: *The fruit of the hadar tree* symbolizes Israel; just as the *etrog* has taste as well as fragrance, so Israel have among them men who possess learning and good deeds. *Branches of palm trees,* too, applies to Israel; as the palm tree [*lulav,* the rabbinic term for the palm branch] has taste but not fragrance, so Israel have among them such as possess learning but not good deeds. *And boughs of thick trees* likewise applies to Israel; just as the myrtle has fragrance but no taste, so Israel have among them such as possess good deeds but not learning. *And willows of the brook* also applies to Israel; just as the willow has no taste and no fragrance, so Israel have among them people who possess neither learning nor good deeds. What then does the Holy One, blessed be He, do to them? To destroy them is impossible. But, says the Holy One, blessed be He, let them all be tied together in one band and they will atone one for another. If you have done so (says God), then at that instant I am exalted. Hence it is written: It is He that built His upper chambers in the heaven (Amos 9:6). When is He exalted? What time they are made into one band; as it says: When He founded His band upon the earth *(ibid.).* Accordingly Moses exhorts Israel: And you shall take on the first day the fruit . . . (Deuteronomy 26:2).

Midrash Rabbah. London: The Soncino Press Ltd.

RECIPE

STUFFED CABBAGE
by Mildred Kessler

2 pounds chopped meat
salt
1 large head of cabbage

Sauce
2–3 small pieces of sour salt
1 8-oz. can of tomato sauce

2 tablespoons brown sugar
1 glass water

Make sauce by combining all ingredients in a large bowl. Season the meat with salt, roll into meat balls. Remove the core off the cabbage, then parboil head, taking off the leaves as they become limp (about 5 minutes). Roll one meatball into one large cabbage leaf or two small ones. Put the stuffed cabbage in roasting pan and cover with sauce. Then sprinkle with paprika, if desired. Cover pan and put on top of stove on high flame until sauce boils. Reduce flame to medium-low and cook for 1 hour. Cook a second hour in oven at 350° (½ hour covered and ½ hour uncovered).

For further information on *Sukot,* see *The Jewish Home,* Book 6.

YOM HA'ATSMAUT

Resource Sheet 73

GLOSSARY

Yom Ha'atsmaut—

Diaspora—

Galut—

Zionism—

Hora—

Resource Sheet 74

THE LAND OF ISRAEL: SELECTED JEWISH SOURCES

FROM THE BIBLE

Genesis 13:14–17.
Isaiah 2:2–4.
Ezekiel 37:1–14.
Amos 9:14, 15.
Psalms 126: 1–6; 137:1–6.

FROM THE DAILY MORNING SERVICE

Bring us in peace from the four corners of the earth, and cause us to walk upright to our land, for You are God who effects salvation.

Sound the great *shofar* for our freedom, and lift the banner to gather our exiles. Gather us together from the four corners of the earth. Blessed are You, Lord, who gathers the dispersed of Your people Israel.

May our eyes see Your return to Zion in mercy. Blessed are You, Lord, who returns Your presence to Zion.

FROM THE SABBATH MORNING SERVICE

When will You reign in Zion? May You dwell there soon, in our days, forever and ever. May You be magnified and sanctified in the midst of Jerusalem, Your city, for all generations and to all eternity.

FROM THE HAGGADAH AND MACHZOR

Next year in Jerusalem *(Leshanah haba'ah birushalayim).*

FROM THE TALMUD

Of the ten measures of wisdom that came down to the world, the Land of Israel took nine and the rest of the world one. Of the ten measures of beauty that came down to the world, Jerusalem took nine and the rest of the world one. (*Kiddushin* 49b)

FROM LITERATURE

If you will it, it is no dream.—Theodor Herzl

Hatikvah (see *Gates of Prayer,* p. 765).

My heart in the East
and I at the farthest West:
how can I taste what I eat or find it sweet
while Zion
is in the cords of Edom and I
bound by the Arab?
Beside the dust of Zion
all the good of Spain is light;
and a light thing to leave it.

Zion, do you ask if the captives are at peace—the few that are left?
I cry out like the jackals when I think of their grief;
but, dreaming of the end of their captivity,
I am like a harp for your songs.

"Jehuda Halevi's Songs to Zion." Reznikoff, Charles. *By the Waters of Manhattan.* New York: New Directions Publishing Corp., 1962.

THE MARCH OF ZIONISM

Important Events		*Zionist Movements and Building of Israel*
		1836: Rabbi Zvi Hirsch Kalischer urges Jewish colonization of Palestine.
	1840	
1848: Jews granted full civil rights in Austro-Hungarian Empire.	**1850**	
	1860	
		1862: Moses Hess urges Jewish Homeland in Palestine.
	1870	1870: Agricultural School, Mikveh Israel, founded in Palestine.
1871: Jews granted full civil rights in Germany. Odessa pogrom.		1878: Petach Tikvah, first agricultural settlement.
1881: Pogroms in Russia. Mass emigration of Jews to Western Hemisphere.	**1880**	1882: Leo Pinsker appeals for return to Palestine. BILU settlements. Rishon Letzion, Ness Tzionah, Zichron Yaakov, Rosh Pinah, Gedera are founded.
1894: The Dreyfus Case in France.	**1890**	1896: Herzl publishes *The Jewish State*. 1897: First Zionist Congress. World Zionist Organization founded in Basle.
1903: Kishinev pogrom (Rumania).	**1900**	1901: Jewish National Fund organized. 1909: Tel Aviv, first Jewish city founded. Deganiah, first kibbutz founded.
1914-1918: World War I, British conquer Palestine from Turks.	**1910**	1910: Ben Yehudah publishes first Hebrew Thesaurus. The birth of modern Hebrew. 1917: Balfour Declaration.
1929: Arab riots in Palestine.	**1920**	1920: Haganah succeeds Hashomer. Histadrut is organized. 1925: Hebrew University opens.
1933: Hitler gains control in Germany. 1936: Arab riots continue. 1939-1945: World War II, almost complete destruction of Europe's Jewry by the Nazis. 1940: British severely restrict Jewish immigration and land purchase.	**1930** **1940**	1937: Proposal for dividing Palestine into Arab and Jewish states. 1943: Warsaw Ghetto Revolt. 1947: UN adopts Partition Plan for Palestine. 1948: Successful War of Independence. Israel becomes an independent state.
	1950	1949: Israel becomes 59th member of the UN. 1956: Successful Sinai Campaign. Access gained to Far East through Eilat.
1967: Egypt, Syria, Jordan provoke war against Israel. 1968: Start of War of Attrition. Israel under continuous Arab terrorist attack. 1973: Yom Kippur War launched by Syria and Egypt.	**1960** **1970**	1961: Millionth immigrant since statehood arrives. Construction of Ashdod port begins. 1967: Israeli victory after six days. Israel occupies Sinai, West Bank, Golan Heights. Jerusalem reunified. Russian Jews begin demanding emigration. 1970: Israel's three millionth citizen arrives. 1975: Start of step-by-step negotiations between Israel and Egypt under US auspices.

Left margin (top): Government anti-Semitism in Russian Empire; Jews impoverished; settlement restricted; pogroms; mass emigration to Western Europe and America. Jews in Western Europe become emancipated and educated and they prosper.

Left margin (bottom): Growth of modern anti-Semitism in Germany, Austria, Poland, Hungary, Russia.

Right margin (top): Development of Yishuv. Jewish self-government, settlement.

Right margin (bottom): State grows and consolidates.

Essrig, Harry, and Segal, Abraham. *Israel Today.* New Edition. New York: Union of American Hebrew Congregations, 1977.

HUMMUS RECIPE

1–2 cloves garlic
1 15½-oz. can chick peas, including liquid in the can
salt to taste
juice of one lemon

3–5 tablespoons tehina (sesame seed paste—available in Middle Eastern or Italian groceries or specialty sections of some markets)

If using a food processor, put garlic in first and mince. Then add all the other ingredients and blend. Serve on a flat plate. If desired, sprinkle some olive oil and paprika on top.

YOM HASHOAH

GLOSSARY

Yom Hashoah—

Shtetl (pl. *Shtetlach*)—

Yiddish—

Mamaloshen—

Pogrom—

Anti-Semitism—

From *Spiritual Resistance: Art from Concentration Camps, 1940–1945.*

THE EXTERMINATION OF JEWS

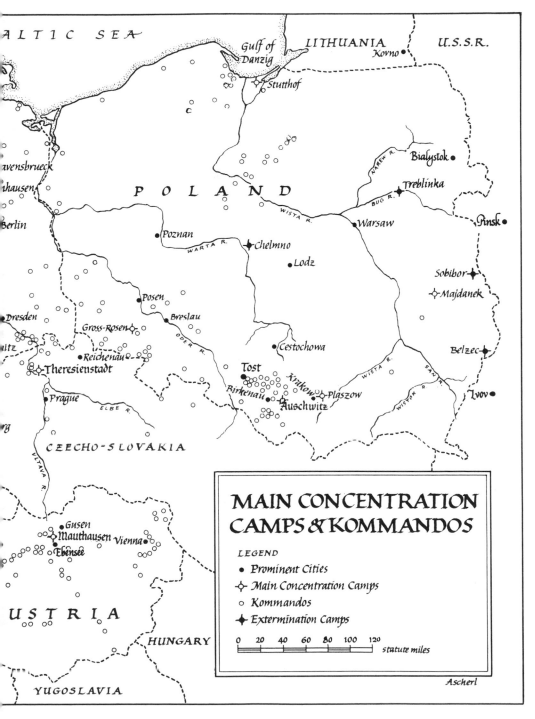

MAIN CONCENTRATION CAMPS & KOMMANDOS

LEGEND
- Prominent Cities
- Main Concentration Camps
- Kommandos
- Extermination Camps

0 20 40 60 80 100 120 statute miles

Ascherl

Union of American Hebrew Congregations, 1981.

THE BUTTERFLY

by Pavel Friedmann
4/6/42

The last, the very last,
So richly, brightly, dazzlingly yellow.
    Perhaps if the sun's tears would sing
    against a white stone. . . .

Such, such a yellow
Is carried lightly 'way up high.
It went away I'm sure because it wished to
    kiss the world goodbye.

For seven weeks I've lived in here,
Penned up inside this ghetto
But I have found my people here.
The dandelions call to me
And the white chestnut candles in the court.
Only I never saw another butterfly.

That butterfly was the last one.
Butterflies don't live in here,
    In the ghetto.

Volavková, Hana, ed. *I Never Saw Another Butterfly.* Translated by Jeanne Nemcova. Second Edition. New York: McGraw-Hill, Inc., 1964.

THE SONG OF THE JEWISH PARTISANS

by Hirsh Glik

Never say that this is the last road, the final way,
Though darkened skies blot out the light of day,
The longed-for hour shall come,
Oh, never fear!
Our tread drums forth the tidings—
We are here!

From greenest palm-land to the land of whitest snow
We are present with our pain and our woe.
And there where every drop of blood was shed,
There will our courage lift its head.

The sun of dawn will yet light our way.
The tragic past will yet fade away,
But if the light should fail to rise for us
Then this song shall tell all ages of our trust.

We wrote this song in blood for all to sing
It is not the carol of a gay bird on the wing.
But amidst crashing walls and fiercely flaming brands
We sang it holding grenades in our hands.

Never say that this is the last road, the final way,
That this is the last time that we shall see the day.
The longed-for hour will come,
Oh, never fear!
Our tread shall roll like thunder—
We are here!

Glik, a partisan killed in 1943, composed this song in his native Yiddish.
It was made the official hymn of the partisans and was translated into many
languages.

Resource Sheet 81

A JEW TODAY

by Elie Wiesel

. . . The Jew who refused death, who refused to believe in death, who chose to marry in the ghetto, to circumcise his son, to teach him the sacred language, to bind him to the threatened and weakened lineage of Israel—that Jew was resisting. The professor or shopkeeper who disregarded facts and warnings and clung to illusion, refusing to admit that people could so succumb to degradation—he, too, was resisting. There was no essential difference between the Warsaw Ghetto fighters and the old men getting off the train in Treblinka: Because they were Jewish, they were all doomed to hate—and death.

In those days, more than ever, to be Jewish signified *refusal.* Above all, it was a refusal to see reality and life through the enemy's eyes—a refusal to resemble him, to grant him that victory, too. . . .

This has always been our way. I remember two episodes. One took place in a train carrying hundreds of Jews to their death. They were pressed together so that they could hardly move or breathe. Suddenly an old rabbi exclaimed, "Today is *Simchat Torah.* Have we forgotten what Jews are ordered to do on *Simchat Torah?*" Somebody had managed to smuggle a small *Sefer Torah* aboard the train; he handed it to the rabbi. And they began to sing, to sway, since they could not dance, and they went on singing and celebrating the Torah, all the while knowing that every motion of the train was bringing them closer to their end.

The second episode took place inside the kingdom of night. In one of the barracks several hundred Jews gathered to celebrate *Simchat Torah.* In the shadow of shadows? Yes—even there. On the threshold of the death chamber? Yes—even there. But, since there was no *Sefer Torah,* how could they organize the traditional procession with the sacred scrolls? As they were trying to solve the problem, an old man—was he really old? the word had no meaning there —noticed a young boy—who was so old, so old—standing there looking on and dreaming. "Do you remember what you learned in *cheder?*" asked the man. "Yes, I do," replied the boy. "Really?" said the man, "you really remember *Shema Yisrael?*" "I remember much more," said the boy. "*Shema Yisrael* is enough," said the man. And he lifted the boy, clasped him in his arms, and began dancing with him—as though *he* were the Torah. And all joined in. They all sang and danced and cried. They wept, but they sang with fervor—never before had Jews celebrated *Simchat Torah* with such fervor.

For, in our tradition, celebration of life is more important than mourning over the dead. When a wedding procession encounters a funeral procession in the street, the mourners must halt so as to allow the wedding party to proceed. Surely you know what respect we show our dead, but a wedding, symbol of life and renewal, symbol of promise too, takes precedence.

Our tradition orders us to affirm life and proclaim hope—always. *Shabbat* interrupts all mourning, being as it is the embodiment of man's hope and his capacity for joy. . . .

Wiesel, Elie. *A Jew Today.* New York: Random House, Inc., 1978.

IF NOT HIGHER

by I.L. Peretz

The rabbi has already been awake for a long time. The Litvak has heard him groaning for a whole hour.

Whoever has heard the Rabbi of Nemirov groan knows how much sorrow for all Israel, how much suffering, lies in each groan. A man's heart might break, hearing it. But a Litvak is made of iron; he listens and remains where he is. The rabbi, long life to him, lies on the bed, and the Litvak under the bed.

Then the Litvak hears the beds in the house begin to creak; he hears people jumping out of their beds, mumbling a few Jewish words, pouring water on their fingernails, banging doors. Everyone has left. It is again quiet and dark; a bit of light from the moon shines through the shutters.

(Afterward the Litvak admitted that when he found himself alone with the rabbi a great fear took hold of him. Goose pimples spread across his skin, and the roots of his earlocks pricked him like needles. A trifle: to be alone with the rabbi at the time of the penitential prayers! But a Litvak is stubborn. So he quivered like a fish in water and remained where he was.)

Finally the rabbi, long life to him, arises. First he does what befits a Jew. Then he goes to the clothes closet and takes out a bundle of peasant clothes: linen trousers, high boots, a coat, a big felt hat, and a long wide leather belt studded with brass nails. The rabbi gets dressed. From his coat pocket dangles the end of a heavy peasant rope.

The rabbi goes out, and the Litvak follows him.

On the way the rabbi stops in the kitchen, bends down, takes an ax from under the bed, puts it in his belt, and leaves the house. The Litvak trembles but continues to follow.

The hushed dread of the Days of Awe hangs over the dark streets. Every once in a while a cry rises from some *minyan* reciting the penitential prayers, or from a sickbed. The rabbi hugs the sides of the streets, keeping to the shade of the houses. He glides from house to house, and the Litvak after him. The Litvak hears the sound of his heartbeats mingling with the sound of the rabbi's heavy steps. But he keeps on going and follows the rabbi to the outskirts of the town.

A small wood stands behind the town.

The rabbi, long life to him, enters the wood. He takes thirty or forty steps and stops by a small tree. The Litvak, overcome with amazement, watches the rabbi take the ax out of his belt and strike the tree. He hears the tree creak and fall. The rabbi chops the tree into logs and the logs into sticks. Then he makes a bundle of the wood and ties it with the rope in his pocket. He puts the bundle of wood on his back, shoves the ax back into his belt, and returns to the town.

He stops at a back street beside a small broken-down shack and knocks at the window.

"Who is there?" asks a frightened voice. The Litvak recognizes it as the voice of a sick Jewish woman.

"I," answers the rabbi in the accent of a peasant.

"Who is I?"

Again the rabbi answers in Russian. "Vassil."

"Who is Vassil, and what do you want?"

"I have wood to sell, very cheap." And, not waiting for the woman's reply, he goes into the house.

The Litvak steals in after him. In the gray light of early morning he sees a poor room with broken, miserable furnishings. A sick woman, wrapped in rags, lies on the bed. She complains bitterly, "Buy? How can I buy? Where will a poor widow get money?"

"I'll lend it to you," answers the supposed Vassil. "It's only six cents."

"And how will I ever pay you back?" said the poor woman, groaning.

"Foolish one," says the rabbi reproachfully. "See, you are a poor sick Jew, and I am ready to trust you with a little wood. I am sure you'll pay. While you, you have such a great and mighty God and you don't trust Him for six cents."

"And who will kindle the fire?" said the widow. "Have I the strength to get up? My son is at work."

"I'll kindle the fire," answers the rabbi.

As the rabbi put the wood into the oven he recited, in a groan, the first portion of the penitential prayers.

As he kindled the fire and the wood burned brightly, he recited, a bit more joyously, the second portion of the penitential prayers. When the fire was set he recited the third portion, and then he shut the stove.

The Litvak who saw all this became a disciple of the rabbi.

And ever after, when another disciple tells how the Rabbi of Nemirov ascends to heaven at the time of the penitential prayers, the Litvak does not laugh. He only adds quietly, "If not higher."

Howe, Irving, and Greenberg, Eliezer, eds. *A Treasury of Yiddish Stories.* Translated by Marie Syrkin. New York: The Viking Press, Inc., 1954.

NOTES ON "IF NOT HIGHER"

Penitential prayers *(Selichot)*—Prayers asking for forgiveness traditionally recited in the predawn hours, during the month of *Elul,* which immediately precedes the High Holy Days.

Rabbi of Nemirov—Chasidic leader whose dynasty was centered in the town of Nemirov. The Chasidim believed that their leaders, or *rebbes,* were invested with special spiritual powers.

Minyan—Literally, a quorum of ten Jews required for public worship service. In this case, the term refers to a group of men who meet every day, morning and evening, to recite the daily prayers.

Days of Awe—The High Holy Day period, beginning with *Rosh Hashanah* and ending with *Yom Kippur.*

Litvak—Literally, a Jew from Lithuania. The stereotype of the Litvak is a person who is an ultrarationalist, steeped in the Talmud and other religio-legal literature.

Resource Sheet 83

IN BLUEBEARD'S CASTLE

by George Steiner

... This is a minority view. Understandably, in an effort to make this insane material susceptible and bearable to reason, sociologists, economists, political scientists have striven to locate the topic in a rational, secular grid. They have investigated the opportunistic sources of Nazi racial theories; the long tradition of petit-bourgeois resentment against a seemingly aloof, prospering minority. They have pointed, rightly, to the psychological, symbolic links between inflationary collapse and the historical associations of Jewry and the money market. There have been penetrating studies of the imperfect, perhaps overhasty assimilation of secularized Jews into the gentile community, an assimilation which produced much of the intellectual genius of modern Europe but also, particularly in Germany, took on the guise of a complex love-hate. Social historians have shown how numerous were the signs of developing hysteria between the Dreyfus affair and the "final solution." Deliberate poisons had been let loose. It has been argued, cogently, that there is an ultimately rational, albeit murderous, motive behind Nazi and Stalinist anti-Semitism: an attempt to get rid of a minority whose inheritance and whose style of feeling make of it a natural milieu for opposition, for potential subversion.

Each of these lines of inquiry is important. Together they make for an indispensable dossier of historical and sociological insight. But the phenomenon, so far as one is able to take any coherent view of it at all, lies far deeper. No historical or social-psychological model put forward until now, no psychopathology of crowd behavior, of the psychic infirmities of individual leaders and killers, no diagnosis of planned hysteria accounts for certain salient features of the problem. These include the active indifference—"active" because "collaboratively unknowing"—of the vast majority of the European population. They include the deliberate decision of the National Socialist regime, even in the final stages of economic warfare, to liquidate the Jews rather than exploit them towards obvious productive and financial ends. Most enigmatic of all, perhaps, is the persistence of virulent anti-Semitism where no Jews or only a handful survive (for example, in Eastern Europe today). The mystery, in the proper theological sense, is one of hatred without present object.

We are not, I believe, dealing with some monstrous accident in modern social history. The Holocaust was not the result of merely individual pathology or of the neuroses of one nation-state. Indeed, competent observers expected the cancer to spread first, and most virulently, in France. We are not—and this is often misunderstood —considering something truly analogous to other cases of massacre, to the murder of the Gypsies or, earlier, of the Armenians. There are parallels in technique and in the idiom of hatred. But not ontologically, not at the level of philosophic intent. That intent takes us to the heart of certain instabilities in the fabric of Western culture, in the relations between instinctual and religious life. Hitler's jibe that "conscience is a Jewish invention" provides a clue.

. . . Monotheism at Sinai, primitive Christianity, messianic socialism: these are the three supreme moments in which Western culture is presented with what Ibsen termed "the claims of the ideal." These are the three stages, profoundly interrelated, through which Western consciousness is forced to experience the blackmail of transcendence. "Surmount yourself. Surpass the opaque barriers of the mind to attain pure abstraction. Lose your life in order to gain it. Give up property, rank, worldly comfort. Love your neighbor as you do yourself—no, much more, for self-love is sin. Make any sacrifice, endure any insult, even self-denunciation, so that justice may prevail." Unceasingly, the blackmail of perfection has hammered at the confused, mundane, egotistical fabric of common, instinctual behavior. Like a shrilling note in the inner ear. Men are neither saints nor ascetics; their imaginings are gross; ordinarily, their sense of the future is the next milestone. But the insistence of the ideal continued, with a terrible, tactless force.

Three times it sounded from the same historical center. (Some political scientists put at roughly 80 percent the proportion of Jews in the ideological development of messianic socialism and communism.) Three times, Judaism produced a summons to perfection and sought to impose it on the current and currency of Western life. Deep loathing built up in the social subconscious murderous resentments. The mechanism is simple but primordial. *We hate most those who hold out to us a goal, an ideal, a visionary promise which, even though we have stretched our muscles to the utmost, we cannot reach, which slips, again and again, just out of range of our racked fingers—yet, and this is crucial, which remains profoundly desirable, which we cannot reject because we fully acknowledge its supreme value. In his* exasperating "strangeness," in his acceptance of suffering as part of a covenant with the absolute, the Jew became, as it were, the "bad conscience" of Western history. In him the abandonments of spiritual and moral perfection, the hypocrisies of an established, mundane religiosity, the absences of a disappointed, potentially vengeful God were kept alive and visible.

When it turned on the Jew, Christianity and European civilization turned on the incarnation—albeit an incarnation often wayward and unaware—of its own best hopes. It is something like this that Kafka meant in his arrogant humble assertion that "he who strikes a Jew strikes down man/mankind" *(den Menschen)*. In the Holocaust there were both a lunatic retribution, a lashing out against intolerable pressures of vision, and a large measure of self-mutilation. The secular, materialist, warlike community of modern Europe sought to extirpate from itself, from its own inheritance, archaic, now ridiculously obsolete, but somehow inextinguishable carriers of the ideal. In the Nazi idiom of "vermin" and "sanitation" there is a brusque insight into the infectious nature of morality. Kill the remembrancer, the claim agent, and you will have canceled the long debt.

The genocide that took place in Europe and the Soviet Union during the period 1935–45 (Soviet anti-Semitism being perhaps the most paradoxical expression of the hatred which reality feels towards failed utopia) was far more than a political tactic, an eruption of lower-middleclass malaise, or a product of declining capitalism. It was no mere secular, socioeconomic phenomenon. It enacted a suicidal impulse in Western civilization. It was an attempt to level the future—or, more precisely, to make history commensurate with the natural savageries, intellectual torpor, and material instincts of unextended man. Using theological metaphors, and there is no need to apologize for them in an essay on culture, the Holocaust may be said to mark a second Fall. We can interpret it as a voluntary exit from the Garden and a programmatic attempt to burn the Garden behind us. Lest its remembrance continue to infect the health of barbarism with debilitating dreams or with remorse.

With the botched attempt to kill God and the very nearly successful attempt to kill those who had "invented" Him, civilization entered, precisely as Nietzsche had foretold, "on night and more night." . . .

Steiner, George. *In Bluebeard's Castle.* New Haven: Yale University Press, 1971.

YOM KIPPUR

Resource Sheet 84

GLOSSARY

Yom Kippur—

Shabbat Shuvah—

Kol Nidrei—

Yizkor—

Yahrzeit Candle—

Resource Sheet 85

AL CHET

MORNING SERVICE

עַל חֵטְא שֶׁחָטָאנוּ לְפָנֶיךָ בִּרְכִילוּת,

Al chet shechatanu lefanecha birchilut

The sin we have committed against You by malicious gossip

עַל חֵטְא שֶׁחָטָאנוּ לְפָנֶיךָ בְּגִלוּי עֲרָיוֹת,

al chet shechatanu lefanecha begilui arayot

the sin we have committed against You by sexual immorality

וְעַל חֵטְא שֶׁחָטָאנוּ לְפָנֶיךָ בְּמַאֲכָל וּבְמִשְׁתֶּה.

ve'al chet shechatanu lefanecha bema'achal uvemishteh.

and the sin we have committed against You by gluttony.

עַל חֵטְא שֶׁחָטָאנוּ לְפָנֶיךָ בְּצָרוּת עָיִן,

Al chet shechatanu lefanecha betsarut ayin

The sin we have committed against You by narrow-mindedness

עַל חֵטְא שֶׁחָטָאנוּ לְפָנֶיךָ בְּכַחַשׁ וּבְכָזָב,

al chet shechatanu lefanecha bechachush uvechazav

the sin we have committed against You by fraud and falsehood

וְעַל חֵטְא שֶׁחָטָאנוּ לְפָנֶיךָ בְּשִׂנְאַת חִנָּם.

ve'al chet shechatanu lefanecha besinat chinam.

and the sin we have committed against You by hating without cause.

עַל חֵטְא שֶׁחָטָאנוּ לְפָנֶיךָ בִּנְטִיַּת גָּרוֹן,

Al chet shechatanu lefanecha bintiyat garon

The sin we have committed against You by our arrogance

עַל חֵטְא שֶׁחָטָאנוּ לְפָנֶיךָ בְּעַזוּת מֶצַח,

al chet shechatanu lefanecha be'azut metsach

the sin we have committed against You by our insolence

וְעַל חֵטְא שֶׁחָטָאנוּ לְפָנֶיךָ בְּקַלּוּת רֹאשׁ.

ve'al chet shechatanu lefanecha bekalut rosh.

and the sin we have committed against You by our irreverence.

עַל חֵטְא שֶׁחָטָאנוּ לְפָנֶיךָ בְּוִדּוּי פֶּה,

Al chet shechatanu lefanecha bevidui peh
The sin we have committed against You by our hypocrisy

עַל חֵטְא שֶׁחָטָאנוּ לְפָנֶיךָ בִּפְלִלוּת,

al chet shechatanu lefanecha bifelilut
the sin we have committed against You by passing judgment on others

וְעַל חֵטְא שֶׁחָטָאנוּ לְפָנֶיךָ בְּנֶשֶׁךְ וּבְמַרְבִּית.

ve'al chet shechatanu lefanecha beneshech uvemarbit.
and the sin we have committed against You by exploiting the weak.

עַל חֵטְא שֶׁחָטָאנוּ לְפָנֶיךָ בְּכַפַּת שֹׁחַד,

Al chet shechatanu lefanecha bechapat shochad
The sin we have committed against You by giving and taking bribes

עַל חֵטְא שֶׁחָטָאנוּ לְפָנֶיךָ בְּיֵצֶר הָרָע,

al chet shechatanu lefanecha beyetser hara
the sin we have committed against You by giving way to our hostile impulses

וְעַל חֵטְא שֶׁחָטָאנוּ לְפָנֶיךָ בְּרִיצַת רַגְלַיִם לְהָרַע.

ve'al chet shechatanu lefanecha beritsat raglayim lehara.
and the sin we have committed against You by running to do evil.

וְעַל כֻּלָּם אֱלוֹהַּ סְלִיחוֹת, סְלַח לָנוּ, מְחַל לָנוּ, כַּפֶּר־לָנוּ!

Ve'al kulam, Elo'ah selichot, selach lanu, mechal lanu, kaper lanu!
For all these sins, O God of mercy, forgive us, pardon us, grant us atonement!

Stern, Chaim, ed. *Gates of Repentance.* New York: Central Conference of American Rabbis, 1978.

Resource Sheet 86

ZOCHRENU LECHAYIM

MORNING SERVICE

בָּרוּךְ אַתָּה, יְיָ אֱלֹהֵינוּ וֵאלֹהֵי אֲבוֹתֵינוּ, אֱלֹהֵי
אַבְרָהָם, אֱלֹהֵי יִצְחָק, וֵאלֹהֵי יַעֲקֹב: הָאֵל הַגָּדוֹל,
הַגִּבּוֹר וְהַנּוֹרָא, אֵל עֶלְיוֹן. גּוֹמֵל חֲסָדִים טוֹבִים,
וְקוֹנֵה הַכֹּל, וְזוֹכֵר חַסְדֵי אָבוֹת, וּמֵבִיא גְאֻלָּה לִבְנֵי
בְנֵיהֶם, לְמַעַן שְׁמוֹ, בְּאַהֲבָה.

*Baruch Atah Adonai Elohenu velohei avotenu Elohei Avraham Elohei
Yitschak velohei Ya'akov: Ha'el hagadol hagibor vehanora El Elyon.
Gomel chasadim tovim vekoneh hakol vezocher chasdei avot umevi
geulah livnei venehem lema'an shemo beahavah.*

Lord, You are the God of all generations: the ones that are past, and
those yet unborn. You are our God.

You are the First; You are the Last; You are the Only One.

You made the earth and brought us forth to dwell in it.

You called Abraham to righteousness, his children to bear witness to Your glory.

You formed us to be a covenant people, eternal as the hosts of
heaven.

O God, You are the Shield of our people, our everlasting light.

זָכְרֵנוּ לְחַיִּים, מֶלֶךְ חָפֵץ בַּחַיִּים, וְכָתְבֵנוּ בְּסֵפֶר
הַחַיִּים, לְמַעַנְךָ אֱלֹהִים חַיִּים. מֶלֶךְ עוֹזֵר וּמוֹשִׁיעַ
וּמָגֵן. בָּרוּךְ אַתָּה, יְיָ, מָגֵן אַבְרָהָם.

*Zochrenu lechayim Melech chafets bachayim vechotvenu besefer ha-
chayim lemu'ancha Elohim chayim. Melech ozer umoshia umagen.
Baruch Atah Adonai magen Avraham.*

Remember us unto life, O King who delights in life, and inscribe us in the Book of Life, for Your sake, O God of life.

Stern, Chaim, ed. *Gates of Repentance.* New York: Central Conference of American Rabbis, 1978.

Resource Sheet 87

AVINU MALKENU

MORNING SERVICE

אָבִינוּ מַלְכֵּנוּ, חָטָאנוּ לְפָנֶיךָ.

Avinu Malkenu chatanu lefanecha.
Our Father, our King, we have sinned before You.

אָבִינוּ מַלְכֵּנוּ, הַחֲזִירֵנוּ בִּתְשׁוּבָה שְׁלֵמָה לְפָנֶיךָ.

Avinu Malkenu hachazirenu bitshuvah shelemah lefanecha.
Our Father, our King, bring us back to You in full repentance.

אָבִינוּ מַלְכֵּנוּ, סְלַח וּמְחַל לְכָל עֲוֹנוֹתֵינוּ.

Avinu Malkenu selach umechal lechol avonotenu.
Our Father, our King, forgive and pardon all our misdeeds.

אָבִינוּ מַלְכֵּנוּ, חֲמוֹל עָלֵינוּ וְעַל עוֹלָלֵינוּ וְטַפֵּנוּ.

Avinu Malkenu chamol alenu ve'al olalenu vetapenu.
Our Father, our King, have compassion on us and on our children.

אָבִינוּ מַלְכֵּנוּ, כַּלֵּה דֶבֶר וְחֶרֶב וְרָעָב מֵעָלֵינוּ.

Avinu Malkenu kaleh dever vecherev vera'av me'alenu.
Our Father, our King, make an end to sickness, war, and famine.

אָבִינוּ מַלְכֵּנוּ, כָּתְבֵנוּ בְּסֵפֶר חַיִּים טוֹבִים.

Avinu Malkenu kotvenu besefer chayim tovim.
Our Father, our King, inscribe us for blessing in the Book of Life.

אָבִינוּ מַלְכֵּנוּ, חַדֵּשׁ עָלֵינוּ שָׁנָה טוֹבָה.

Avinu Malkenu chadesh alenu shanah tovah.
Our Father, our King, let the new year be a good year for us.

אָבִינוּ מַלְכֵּנוּ, עֲשֵׂה עִמָּנוּ לְמַעַן שְׁמֶךָ.

Avinu Malkenu aseh imanu lema'an shemecha.
Our Father, our King, help us to exalt Your name in the world.

אָבִינוּ מַלְכֵּנוּ. קַבֵּל בְּרַחֲמִים וּבְרָצוֹן אֶת־תְּפִלָּתֵנוּ.

Avinu Malkenu kabel berachamim uveratson et tefilatenu.
Our Father, our King, in Your mercy accept our prayer.

אָבִינוּ מַלְכֵּנוּ, חָנֵּנוּ וַעֲנֵנוּ, כִּי אֵין בָּנוּ מַעֲשִׂים, עֲשֵׂה
עִמָּנוּ צְדָקָה וָחֶסֶד וְהוֹשִׁיעֵנוּ.

Avinu Malkenu chonenu va'anenu ki en banu ma'asim aseh imanu tsedakah vachesed vehoshienu.

Our Father, our King, be gracious and answer us, for we have little merit. Treat us generously and with kindness, and be our help.

Stern, Chaim, ed. *Gates of Repentance.* New York: Central Conference of American Rabbis, 1978.

Resource Sheet 88

YOM KIPPUR EVE BLESSINGS

After the meal, it is customary to light the *Yahrzeit* candle(s) in memory of the departed. No blessing is said.

Then, the *Yom Kippur* candles are lit and the following blessings are recited.

The holiest day of the year is about to begin. Let us use it well. May it be for each one of us a day of renewal. May it help us to overcome what is evil in us and to strengthen what is good. May it bring us closer to one another and make us more loyal to our community, our faith, and our God.

בָּרוּךְ אַתָּה, יְיָ אֱלֹהֵינוּ, מֶלֶךְ הָעוֹלָם, אֲשֶׁר קִדְּשָׁנוּ בְּמִצְוֹתָיו,
וְצִוָּנוּ לְהַדְלִיק נֵר שֶׁל (שַׁבָּת וְשֶׁל) יוֹם הַכִּפּוּרִים.

Baruch Atah Adonai Elohenu Melech ha'olam asher kideshanu bemitsvotav vetsivanu lehadlik ner shel (Shabbat veshel) Yom Hakippurim.

Blessed is the Lord our God, Ruler of the universe, by whose *mitzvot* we are hallowed; who commands us to kindle the lights of (*Shabbat* and) the Day of Atonement.

בָּרוּךְ אַתָּה, יְיָ אֱלֹהֵינוּ, מֶלֶךְ הָעוֹלָם, שֶׁהֶחֱיָנוּ וְקִיְּמָנוּ וְהִגִּיעָנוּ
לַזְּמַן הַזֶּה.

Baruch Atah Adonai Elohenu Melech ha'olam shehecheyanu vekiyemanu vehigianu lazeman hazeh.

Blessed is the Lord our God, Ruler of the universe, for giving us life, for sustaining us, and for enabling us to reach this season.

Stern, Chaim, ed. *Gates of the House.* New York: Central Conference of American Rabbis, 1976.

Resource Sheet 89

MEALS BEFORE AND AFTER THE FAST

It is traditional that the pre-fast dinner includes foods which are not heavily spiced or salted—chicken soup with *matzah* balls, boiled chicken, salad, baked apples, honey cake, etc.

To break the fast, many people prefer a "dairy" meal—herring, lox, tuna salad, rolls, bagels, cream cheese, fruits, juices, coffee, and tea.

For further information on *Yom Kippur,* see *The Jewish Home,* Book 4.

Credits

We wish to acknowledge with gratitude the following authors and publishers for permission to reprint material from their works:

Behrman House, Inc.: From *The Bar Mitzvah Treasury,* edited by Azriel Eisenberg. Copyright © 1952 by Azriel Eisenberg; from *A Maimonides Reader,* edited by Isadore Twersky. Copyright © 1972 by Isadore Twersky. Both are reprinted by permission of Behrman House, Inc., publishers.

Central Conference of American Rabbis: From *Gates of Mitzvah,* edited by Simeon J. Maslin. Copyright © 1979; from *Gates of the House,* edited by Chaim Stern. Copyright © 1976; from *Rabbi's Manual.* Copyright © 1961. All are copyright by the Central Conference of American Rabbis and reprinted by permission.

Central Conference of American Rabbis and Union of Liberal and Progressive Synagogues, London: From *Gates of Repentance,* edited by Chaim Stern. Copyright © 1978. Reprinted by permission of the Central Conference of American Rabbis.

Dilia, Prague: "The Butterfly," by Pavel Friedmann, from *I Never Saw Another Butterfly.* Reprinted with permission of Dr. H. Volavková, editor.

Harcourt Brace Jovanovich, Inc.: From *A Believing Jew,* by Milton Steinberg. Copyright © 1951 by Edith Steinberg; renewed 1979 by Jonathan Steinberg and David Joel Steinberg. Reprinted by permission of Harcourt Brace Jovanovich, Inc.

Hebrew Union College Press: From *Recent Reform Responsa,* by Solomon B. Freehof. Copyright © 1963. Reprinted with permission from the Hebrew Union College Press.

Holt, Rinehart and Winston, Publishers: From *The Jews of Silence,* by Elie Wiesel. Translated by Neal Kozodoy. Copyright © 1966 by Holt, Rinehart and Winston. Reprinted by permission.

The Jewish Publication Society of America: From *The First Jewish Catalog,* compiled and edited by Richard Siegel, Michael Strassfeld, and Sharon Strassfeld. Copyright © 1973; from *The Second Jewish Catalog,* compiled and edited by Michael Strassfeld and Sharon Strassfeld. Copyright © 1976. Both are copyright and used through the courtesy of the Jewish Publication Society of America.

The Jewish Reconstructionist Foundation, Inc.: "Why No Christmas Tree: A letter from a Jewish Convert to Her Christian Mother"